Perfect Phrases for Executive Presentations

Also available from McGraw-Hill

Perfect Phrases for Performance Reviews by Douglas Max and Robert Bacal

Perfect Phrases for Performance Goals by Douglas Max and Robert Bacal

Perfect Solutions for Difficult Employee Situations by Sid Kemp

Perfect Phrases for Customer Service by Robert Bacal

Perfect Phrases for Business Proposals and Business Plans by Don Debelak

Perfect Phrases for the Sales Call by William T. Brooks

Perfect Phrases for Executive Presentations

**Hundreds of Ready-to-Use Phrases to Use to
Communicate Your Strategy and Vision
When the Stakes Are High**

Alan M. Perlman

McGraw-Hill

New York Chicago San Francisco Lisbon
London Madrid Mexico City Milan New Delhi
San Juan Seoul Singapore Sydney Toronto

The **McGraw·Hill** Companies

Copyright © 2006 by The McGraw-Hill Companies, Inc. Printed in the United States of America. Except as permitted under the United States Copyright Act of 1976, no part of this publication may be reproduced or distributed in any form or by any means, or stored in a database or retrieval system, without the prior written permission of the publisher.

   2 3 4 5 6 7 8 9 0   FGR/FGR   0 9 8 7 6

ISBN 0-07-146763-7

This is a *CWL Publishing Enterprises Book* produced for McGraw-Hill by CWL Publishing Enterprises, Inc., Madison, Wisconsin, www.cwlpub.com.

McGraw-Hill books are available at special quantity discounts to use as premiums and sales promotions, or for use in corporate training programs. For more information, please write to the Director of Special Sales, Professional Publishing, McGraw-Hill, Two Penn Plaza, New York, NY 10121-2298. Or contact your local bookstore.

 This book is printed on recycled, acid-free paper containing a minimum of 50% recycled, de-inked fiber.

Contents

Contents

Contents

Contents

Contents

Contents

Contents

Contents

Contents

Part Four. Specific Speech Situations   105

28. Keynote Speeches (Internal or External)   107

29. Panel Remarks   109

30. IPO Announcements   110

Contents

Contents

Contents

Contents

Contents

Contents

Preface

"Perfect phrases" is quite an ambitious claim. How perfect are the phrases in this book? They're perfect grammatically, and they're perfectly understandable. And—except where noted—they're perfectly appropriate for the occasion and context for which I'm recommending them.

But they may not be perfect for every occasion or speaker. Each paragraph between double quotes (" ") is a connected whole, but you may want to take pieces of it or use only a section. I've written many of the paragraphs so that you can pull out sentences or groups of sentences that will stand on their own. Be sure to edit your revised version carefully; make sure you haven't introduced errors of grammar or logic.

The phrases can also be quite flexible. In italics and brackets *[like this]*, you'll find my comments and suggestions as to how you can insert material and develop particular points. The words and phrases in brackets alone [like this] or separated by slashes—like/this—are my suggested alternative words and phases; they're different ways of saying the same thing. Check your thesaurus for alternatives to my suggestions.

I've used a generic, straight-down-the-middle speechwriting style, but it may not be perfect for you. Feel free to alter the phrases so that they fit your exact speaking style, as long as you don't introduce any errors or inconsistencies. Again, edit your revised version. Be careful not to introduce inappropriate business jargon or impersonal expressions. For advice on developing a conversational, personal speechwriting style, see Section 46.

The book will help you even if you wind up saying something completely different from the suggested phrases. The items that follow each lower-case letter—a), b), etc.—are a key resource: they are the *relevant speech themes*—the topics it's appropriate to talk about and the points you might want to make in particular situations. But you can also think of them as thought-starters to generate other things you might want to say.

The phrases in this book are perfect as examples of what you could say. Whichever of these phrases you choose to use, make sure that they are fully appropriate to your specific situation.

Using This Book

This book is organized around speech types. Parts Two through Five deal with the main types of speeches and presentations most executives will be involved in. Within each part, you will find numbered sections that break down these types of speeches by audience and situation. I've put these sections in the approximate order in which might occur in a speech, with sample phrases you can use to effectively make your points and connect with your audience. So along with key points and phrases, the book shows how to effectively organize your speech.

Part One explains the characteristics of a great speech. I give you specific advice that will make your presentation memorable for you and your audience. Parts Six and Seven give you strategies for using language that will help you with specific audiences: non-native English speakers, your employees, and primarily female audiences. Part Seven gives advice for effectively delivering your well-written speech.

Thanks

For a long time, there's been a debate among speechwriters over whether speakers should conclude with "Thank you" or "Thank you very much"—or just end the speech. After all, if we write the ending effectively enough, won't everybody know it's the end?

After years of pondering this question, I've come down on the side of "Thank you."

There's nothing wrong with one final expression of appreciation to your listeners for giving you their time (after perhaps braving the traffic, weather, or other obstacles) and attention (which they divert from a dozen other distractions, though probably not always successfully). These are great gifts, and one must take every opportunity to express gratitude for them.

Thank you very much for reading this book and for letting me help you be a better communicator.

If you have any questions or comments, please e-mail me at info@alanperlman.com.

Perfect Phrases for
Executive Presentations

Part One

What Makes a Great Speech?

Would you like to make your next speech—and every speech after that—great? It's not easy—but it's simple.

Your goal is to make your listeners like you and bond with you, even as they accept the argument, information, inspiration, or whatever you're offering. If you can do that and thus provide real "audience value," you've given a great speech—the exact speech that the occasion calls for, a speech in which the audience's needs are fully met and the speaker's goals are fully achieved.

I don't think some speeches regarded as great by historians are all that great *as speeches*, although some definitely are. Where perceptions are concerned, it's hard to separate the effect of context. Great speeches are associated with great events, although that's not always the case. In a war or other crisis, it's often (unfortunately) all too easy to decide what to say and how to say it.

But how do you achieve everyday greatness? By doing what all the best speakers do: combine outstanding delivery with outstanding content; build audience rapport even as you deliver the message that the audience is to accept. Part One gives you some proven ways to do that.

1. Quickly Establish a Link, a Relationship with Your Audience

Thank the person who introduced you. Display a positive attitude, energy, an eagerness to communicate—all of which makes the audience want to hear you. (Don't overdo it. The only reason I bring up the subject of enthusiasm is that too many speakers lack the initial animation that arouses listeners and makes them want to pay attention.) Express enthusiasm for your topic. Sincerely tell your listeners why you're glad to be there—unless it's a serious event. (Most of the ones in this book aren't.) Find more than one reason if you can. Your last one could be the topic of your speech or lead into it:

- "I'm delighted to have this opportunity to share some thoughts on a subject I'm passionate about: *[topic]*."
- "Good morning/afternoon/evening, everyone. It's good to see you all, and I'm delighted that *[person who invited you]* asked me to come and talk to you today/tonight."
- "Many speakers like to start off by saying what a pleasure it is to be where they happen to be. But in this case, it's not just 'a' pleasure, but two—a doubleheader, if you will *[or "tripleheader," if you have three reasons to be glad to be there.]*"
- "Good morning/afternoon/evening, and thank you all for coming. To all of you—old friends and new faces alike—let me say how delighted ... and *honored* ... I am to be here with you today." *[Explain why.]*
- "Good morning/afternoon/evening and welcome, everyone. I'm delighted to see that so many of you could be with us today/tonight."

3

- "I know how much you all have on your plates. We wouldn't ask you to take time from your busy schedules unless the matter were truly important. And it is."
- *[To open a conference:]* "Good morning/afternoon/evening, and thank you for asking me to be a part of this important event."
- "Thank you and good evening. I'm truly honored by the invitation to address this distinguished audience. And I've been looking forward to this occasion for many weeks. In fact, when we started kicking around ideas for this speech, one of my colleagues remarked that 'asking *[your name]* to talk about *[your subject]* is like asking the Pope to talk about God.'"
- "Thanks, *[person who introduced you]*, and good morning/afternoon/evening, everyone. This is a great turnout. Let me tell you first off what a pleasure it is to get together with such a large group of fellow members of the *[name of company/organization]* family."

Bond with the listeners by working from what you and they have in common. It probably has to do with why you're there. At least mention or refer to it in some positive and complimentary way. You can even build your speech around that commonality, if it's appropriate.

Within that shared context, what is your relationship to your listeners? Older mentor? Peer? Professional expert? Industry/organizational/workshop leader? Fellow graduate from an institution? Supporter of a cause?

Be conscious of how you relate to your listeners (see if you can verbalize it to yourself), because that relationship influences what you choose to talk about—to the extent that you have a choice—and how you talk about it. As you think about wording and delivery, strive for as much true equality as possible, without downplaying the power differences between you and the audience. (For advice on selecting topics, see my book, *Writing Great Speeches: Professional Techniques You Can Use* [Boston: Allyn and Bacon, 1997], Chapter 1. For advice on clarity and style, see Chapters 7 and 8 respectively.)

Much of what I'll tell you about how to compose your speech will already include audience sensitivity.

When you use clear, simple language (as in the Perfect Phrases) and present a speech that has a discernable structure and purpose, you show the members of the audience that you care about them and that you'll make it as easy and enjoyable as possible for them to hear what you have to say.

Similarly, a gracious opening, a strong closing, a show of enthusiasm for an organization's mission, a willingness to share credit, a focus on "audience value"—these and other examples and techniques that I'll show you are all implicit signs that you care about whether your listeners understand you … and about whether you connect with them.

Note: If your topic is controversial, try to identify the common ground.

Example:

- "Reasonable people can agree on goals but still have honest disagreements on how to reach them. It's not a conflict between good and evil. Let's just acknowledge that we are all in favor of *[mutual goal]*."

2. Speak *to* and *with* the Audience: Make Your Speech Interactive

Even though a speech is essentially a monologue, it is also a live communication and thus bears some resemblance to a conversation. Successful speeches simulate this conversational element and include the audience through the skillful use of interactive language. Here are some ways to do this.

Rhetorical questions. These are questions to which there is no answer or to which the answer is obvious. For example, you might state a questionable or outlandish idea, then say something like "Do you think anyone would believe that?"

Question and answer. This is a variation on the rhetorical question. Ask the question as if you expect the audience to answer it and then give the answer yourself.

- "To give customers what they want, we have to understand what it is. So what do we mean by 'value' [or other concept]?" *[Follow with explanation.]*
- "Is this unrealistic? I don't think so."
- "Why are we having this conference/meeting? And what do we hope to accomplish?" *[Follow with explanation.]*
- "But how do people make their vision a reality? How do we achieve all those lofty goals we set for ourselves?" *[Follow with explanation.]*
- "How does it do that? Well, …." *[Explain.]*
- "With all of these challenges, can we be even more successful in the future? Absolutely!"
- "What's going to happen now? Well, …."

Respond to what you take to be the audience's silent reaction.
- "Yes, I know what you're thinking—it's risky to do something radically different."

- "Maybe you're a bit skeptical about all of this. You're wondering ...." [Be specific about the skepticism, then give reasons why they shouldn't be skeptical.]

- "Well, I hope my facts and figures have startled you a little, because unless we do something about them ...." [Discuss negative consequences.]

- "Hopefully, you're no longer thinking, '[audience's original perspective],' ... but rather '[perspective to which you hope to convert them].'"

- [After announcing a vision, goal, or desired outcome:] "Sounds great, doesn't it?"

- "I hope I've left each of you asking yourselves one question: '[hypothetical question, e.g., "Am I challenging myself enough to____?"].' I really don't know; each of you has to answer it for yourself."

Use conversational tags. These can be attached to any sentence you want to emphasize.

- "I would expect more, *wouldn't you?*"

Call for a physical response from the audience (voice vote, show of hands, etc.).

Call for a silent response:

- "Do you want to be engaged in *[name of project or venture]*? I hope you mentally answered 'yes'—or maybe even something stronger."

Frame your sentences so that you include the audience:

- "I'm sure many of you have read the article and formed your own opinions." (*Rather than* "Many people have read and reacted to the article.")

  Interactive alternatives:

  – "I'll bet most of you have read the article, right?" [Wait

for audience's silent assent.]
- "How many here have read the article?" *[Wait for show of hands.]*
- "I'm sure all of you/us are aware that the article says that ...."
- "Now, I don't expect all of this to happen overnight— and neither should you." (*Rather than* "These objectives will probably not be achieved over the short term.")
- "You know the problem. It's simply that ...." (*Rather than* "The problem is simply that ....")
- "Just look at what it's already helped us do." (*Rather than* "It's helped us to achieve a great deal.")

Address the audience directly:
- "Don't you find it amazing that ...?"
- "Think about it: ...." *[Make important or provocative point.]*
- "Consider this: ..." *[Make important or provocative point.]*

Invite the audience to share your reaction or thought processes:
- "Think back to our first meeting/conference/etc. What was your most powerful impression? I know what *mine* was: ...."

The level and type of interactivity depend on the topic and the occasion. Use your sensitivity. But note that even in the most serious of speeches there are opportunities to address and include the audience.

3. Begin Right Away and Make Your Purpose Clear at the Outset

Make sure the audience is quiet. Then minimize any initial chitchat, joke telling, and so on. Get right to the point. A short personal anecdote related to the topic of your speech is OK. A short personal anecdote that reflects positively on the organization and leads into your topic is even better. Then get into your main topic:

- "Today I've been asked to talk about/I want to talk about/I'll be talking about ...."
- "I have three different, but related tasks/agenda items this morning/afternoon/etc., so let me get right to them. First ...."
- *[To new hires:]* "In the next few minutes, I'd like to intro-duce—or, if you're a transfer, *re*introduce—you to our com-pany. I'll talk about who we are, where we're going, and how we plan to get there."

Consider stating your purpose in terms of the intended result:

- "My objective is to give you an overview of ...."
- "Today I want to acquaint you with ...."
- "By the time I'm done today, I hope you'll be convinced [*or* as convinced as I am] that ...."
- "I'd like to present you with some really fascinating new information on *[topic]*—information that may change your perspective on ...."
- "I think that by the time I'm done, you'll be as excited as I am about ...."
- "I'm here today to deliver a warning."
- "By the time I'm finished, you'll have a better understand-ing of ...."

- "And when I'm done, I hope you'll have a renewed sense of confidence in your abilities to manage *[difficult/challenging issue],* because that is what we urgently need you to do."

Here are some other suggestions for beginning your speech.

Thank the audience for being there:
- "It's great to see you all … and thank you *so* much for taking time out of your busy schedules to be with us this morning/afternoon/etc.!"

If you're kicking off a conference, express high hopes:
- "I was thinking of giving our conference an appropriate subtitle, something like 'Two Days *[or length of conference]* That Will Change Your Life.'Then I had second thoughts; it sounded a bit too ambitious. But frankly, it does represent my hopes: I do want the next two days to change at least a part of your life. And in the next few minutes, I'll explain how—and why—that can happen."

Tell the audience that you want to get to know them better:
- "Since you and I don't often come face-to-face in an open forum, one of my key action items is for us to get better acquainted. We need to get closer to each other, as people and as professionals. And we need to understand, even better than we do now, the challenges—and the opportunities—that we face today and throughout the rest of this decade." *[You might add:* "So let me start the get-acquainted process by telling you, from my experience and observations across the organization, what I know about *you." You would then compliment audience on their talents and accomplishments by speaking in terms of abilities that enabled them to do what they've done.]*

If you're speaking at a multi-speaker event, relate the content of your speech to that of the previous speaker:

■ "*[Speaker]* told you *[whatever he/she said]*. Now I'm going to talk about *[your topic]* and how it relates to *[previous topic]*."

Make a complimentary remark about the person who invited you:

■ "Back in *[month/year]*, I accepted an invitation from *[person]* to come talk to you today. Now, *[person]* is the kind of person who could sell a screen door to a submarine captain. He/She is *very* persuasive! So when he/she asked me to speak at *[name of this event]*, I was only too happy to oblige."

Use the wording of your assigned topic as a springboard to your main idea:

■ "You've asked me to speak on 'Training for the New Technologies.'' For'—that's the key concept. As the technological strength of our company grows, so must its collective brainpower. Microprocessors and neurons—our success depends on both."

Convey a sense of importance and urgency by expressing strong feelings about the speech topic:

■ "I'm pleased to have this opportunity to offer a few thoughts on a subject that's of intense and immediate interest to all of us in *[industry]*—and that *I* personally feel very strongly about, too."

If speaking about an acknowledged issue, don't spend time explaining it or its importance:

■ "You've heard of speakers who supposedly need no introduction. Well, this is a *speech* that needs no introduction. I don't want open with a joke or a funny story because our subject is anything but humorous. And I certainly don't need to start off with alarming statistics to grab your attention and awaken you to the fact there's a problem. You already know …." *[Mention the problem briefly.]*

Emphasize the value of your personal experience with a much-discussed topic:

- "Oftentimes, what we need is not so much to be *taught* as to be *reminded* of what we already know, especially if we can see it through the lens of someone else's experience. And that's the spirit in which I want to talk to you today/tonight."

If you're discussing implementing what everyone realizes is a good idea:

- "*[Topic]* is one of those 'Of course!' ideas—both profound and obvious at the same time." *[Segue into discussing implementation.]*
- "*[Topic]* is an idea whose time has not only come, but—in reality—is long overdue." *[Segue into discussing implementation.]*

If you're trying to simplify an issue on which much has been said and written:

- "Is *[topic]* really that complicated? Maybe it's like weight loss: we have thousands of books on the subject, but the bottom line, really, is 'eat less, exercise more, and you'll be as thin as your heredity allows you to be.' Let's assume, for the sake of argument, that *[topic]*, at bottom, really *is* simple, and that if we understand just a few things about it, we'll be better equipped to make our way through those thousands of books on it. So if there were just a few keys to understanding *[topic]*, what would they be?"

If you're going to tell the listeners something they probably don't know:

- ■ "I'd like to begin with a little eye-opener. No, I'm not going to be passing out Bloody Marys. It's not that kind of eye-opener. It's the other kind—the enlightenment that comes from finding out something you didn't know before."

If you want to generate interest in a highly technical topic with hidden implications for the audience:

- ■ "Admittedly, studying the minutiae of *[topic]* is about as interesting as watching paint dry—*unless* the paint is on your living room wall and it's the wrong color. Then you might be *very* interested! That, metaphorically/symbolically, is what might happen over the next few years."

If you have discomfiting information or bad news, get right to it:

- ■ "There are some troublesome concerns, some 'maybe-you-didn't-realize' facts that I'd like to pass on to you—some eye-opening realities that should make us all stop and think very soberly about the future of our company and about the way we do business."

- ■ "Good morning/afternoon, and thank you all for being here. I have a difficult job to do today, and the best way to do it is to come right to the point: I'm truly sorry to have to tell you that …. *[Toward the end, repeat your regrets:]* Again, let me say how much I regret having to bring you this news today."

If your speech is a conference kickoff or keynote, close by telling what you hope the audience will gain from the conference:

- ■ "All of which brings me to the purposes of our conference and to what I hope will happen in the next two days

13

[or length of conference]."

If your speech closes a conference, tell what you hope the audience got out of it:

■ "I hope it's been a useful, stimulating, and informative day/week/etc. for all of you. I hope you now know what strategic objectives you'll pursue, what policies you'll implement, and what resources will enable you to achieve everything you've set out to do."

4. Give Your Speech a Simple and Easily Perceivable Organization

I can't overemphasize this: keep it simple. Almost all speeches contain far too much information and go way beyond the audience's attention span and retention capability. Confine yourself to a very few points that relate to your central purpose.

Your speech will be even better if your content is in some sort of logical sequence that the audience can follow. For example, start with events/facts/experiences/trends, discuss their implications, and then make some predictions, so there's a story arc for the audience to follow.

Announce the Structure of Your Speech at the Outset

- "Let me give you a little detail on what a great year it's been. Then I'll talk about where we go from here. I'll finish up with some comments on what you, as *[audience's title/specialty/profession]*, can do to make next year even better."
- "First, I'll discuss *[topic #1]*. Then I'll briefly review *[topic #2]*. And I'll finish up with some comments on *[topic #3]*."
- "In the next few minutes, I'll first describe *[topic #1]*. I'll then explain *[topic #2]* and I'll finish with a brief review of *[topic #3]*."

One possibility is to organize your speech around different perspectives coming from the same person:

- "Today, even though I'll be giving only one speech, I'll be speaking to you in three different roles—as a consumer, an American, and a manager."

Another approach is to construct the speech around "perception" versus "reality" (you're presenting the reality, of course) or the "myths" and "facts" of a particular topic:

- "Today I'm going to be sharing with you some myths and facts about *[topic]*. Now don't get me wrong: I think mythology can be delightful. It gives us gods and goddesses, heroes, and wondrous events that, if you analyze them properly, can tell us a lot about how people explain why things are the way they are. You see, their myths are only mythical to us. We have better explanations for what's happening and why."

Mark Your Transitions

During your speech, keep the audience abreast of where you are in your discussion. Use verbal signals (or "signposts") to mark transitions in your thought process. Here are some general examples:

- "I would also urge you to ...."
- "Another key to realizing your vision is to ...."
- "Let me move on now to the second/third/etc. part of my presentation."
- "Let me give you a brief case study."
- "Let's spend a few moments reviewing the numbers."
- "This is important for several reasons."
- "Now let me move on to our next action item: ...."
- "Action Item #2 is ...."
- "Let me move on to the second step we have to take."
- "The other/another factor/problem/challenge/etc. is that ...."
- "Something else we've learned from our experience is that ...."
- "Now let me turn to the second question/next point I'd like to discuss this morning: ...."

- "That brings me to the second thing I'd like you to do."
- "Well, how about the third requirement: *[requirement]*?"
- "All of which leads quite naturally to a discussion of *[your next topic]*."
- "Our project turned out to have much wider implications." *[Explain implications.]*
- "Let me close this portion of my presentation with a general remark or two on what we've gained—and the benefits we expect to realize."
- "Let me finish up with some comments on what's ahead. I can sum it up in six words: more of the same, but tougher."
- *[To introduce a list of accomplishments:]* "We have a very full plate, but we feel good about what we've been able to get done."
- *[After listing accomplishments, to provide closure:]* "All in all, impressive numbers and remarkable accomplishments, no doubt about it."
- "I hope it's clear by now that …."
- "Now here's one more fact about *[topic]*: …."
- "Our second strategy/third priority/etc. is to …."
- "I've just given you two examples of …."
- "OK, now let's talk about …."
- *[To introduce preliminary results:]* "It's an evolutionary process, and there's much more we can do. In fact, I often feel we've only taken a few steps of a very long journey. But even at this point, …." *[Lead into summary of results so far.]*

One very helpful signpost is the kind that summarizes the discussions so far and points to where the speech is going from there:

- "I've pointed out some of the relevant realities of our era/environment. Now let me set out the issues that I think are pivotal for the future."

- "But I'm talking about more than competence and skill, important as those are."

- "So far, I've talked about *[topic #1]*. But what about *[topic #2]*?"

- "At this point, we were making good progress in *[your goals]*. But we knew there was more we could do."

- "Experience is a harsh teacher, and indeed, we've learned a lot." *[Follow with lessons learned.]*

- "So our past and present have much in common. But what about the future? What are the goals and issues that bind us together?"

- "With all of that as background, let me now turn to this/last year's results."

- "I've talked about *[topic #1]* and *[topic #2]*. Now let me acquaint you with *[topic #3]*."

If part or all of your speech is a chronological account, use signposts like these:

- "Let me start by bringing you up to date with a quick overview of our progress last year."

- "First, a bit of history, to let you know far we've come in just a couple of years *[or whatever time interval]*."

- "Let me start with a flashback to the '70s/'80s/etc."

- *[To skip forward in time:]* "OK, now let's fast-forward to the 1990s."

- *[To identify events that happened at or around the same time:]* "Now, while all of this was going on …."

- *[To conclude a chronological account:]* "And at this brings us up to the present/last year/etc."

Use signposts to signal to the audience that you are adding material on the same subject *from the same point of view*.

To connect items you approve of:
- "Another step in the right direction is ...."
- "Another reason why *[topic X]* is important is that ...."
- "Finally, two more pieces of good news: ...."

To transition from one recommendation to another:
- "I would also urge you to ...."

To transition from one conclusion to another:
- "A third conclusion, which flows right out of the previous one: ...."

To introduce and highlight what you consider the most effective action you're taking or recommending:
- "The biggest bang of all will come from ...."

To introduce and highlight a significant lesson:
- "I come now to the most important learning of all: ...."

To introduce your main theme:
- "This brings me to the core of my message today: ...."

Changing from One Perspective to Another

On the other hand, be especially careful to let the audience know when you're moving from one point of view on the subject to another. Here are some possibilities.

To transition from facts to causes:
- "There are specific reasons why all of this has happened."

To transition from critique to recommendation(s), from vision to action, or from problem(s) to solution(s):
- "Now, it's not enough to just oppose the other guy's position. You have to be *for* something."
- "So much for the problems. Now let me move on to the fixes."

- "Well, you've listened patiently to all of our dreams and schemes, and eventually all of it will indeed happen."

To transition from description to evaluation:
- "This is a very important development." *[Explain why.]*

To transition from news/announcement/information to prediction:
- "What's going to happen now? Well, ... "

To transition from concept to application:
- "Well, so much for the background and the conceptual framework of *[concept]*. Now let's see how this idea has actually worked [for us]."

To transition from concept to example(s)/detail(s):
- "[Well, so much for generalities.] Now let me get specific."
- "Let me give you a little detail on .... "
- "Now let me go back and elaborate on each of these ideas."

To transition from lessons/conclusions to problems:
- "Along with the lessons we've learned and the conclusions we've come to, I'd like to highlight some issues to be avoided/problems we're going to have to grapple with."

To transition from narrative account to lessons learned/ audience value:
- "Well, so much for history. What have we learned? And what would I hope that you take away from this presentation?"
- "I think our experience has some lessons for any company in tough times, so let me tell you what they are."

To transition from accomplishments to results:
- "Even though there's much more to do, the results so far have been impressive."

To transition from strategies/plans to desired outcomes:
- "Well, those are our objectives—what we want to do—and our strategies—how we want to do it. But what does it all lead to? What do we hope will be the operating outcomes—the actual result of our efforts to add value to the organization/drive the business forward to [goal]?"

To transition from report to action/improvement items:
- "Now: how do we go from good to great? What's it going to take to get us the rest of the way to [goal]?"
- "It was, as the song says, a very good year. But we won't stop there."
- "Well, where do we go from here?"

To transition from topics more distant from location and/or knowledge/experience:
- "Now let me come closer to home—[both] [geographically] [and] [in terms of my own knowledge/experience] [—]and talk a little about [new topic]."

To transition from success stories to tasks remaining:
- "This is all very positive, but there's still more to do."

To reintroduce or refocus on your main theme:
- "Which brings me back to the key message I have for you today: ...."
- "But let me get back to the reason why I'm here."

To transition from information to implications:
- "I've discussed the trends that are shaping our industry. What do they mean for us?"

You can probably add just as many of your own examples—ones that you will create to fit the situation. Every time you change the subject—even a little—consider whether you need to explicitly take your audience along with you.

5. Practice Authenticity

Authenticity makes a speech believable and persuasive. How do you develop and display it?

A speech is, to some extent, a personal statement to the audience. So consider using a personal anecdote or story to illustrate your points or to begin or end your speech. You thus prove that you know, through direct experience, what you're talking about. The story doesn't have to be funny—just relevant. The technique works even in serious speeches.

You can set up your anecdote by making your point first and then saying, "When I say that, I'm not just guessing or hoping—I *know* it's true, because ..." and going into your story.

As with all techniques, use this one judiciously: less is more. If you're going to be humorous, stick mainly to stories that are mildly self-deprecating—the safest and best kind of humor. You thus prove that you are fallible, like everyone else.

Strive for authenticity everywhere in your communications.

Use your own words. Don't use my phrases if they don't sound natural; rewrite them. Don't use business or technical jargon and buzzwords if the occasion requires plain talk. Speak and write in a personal style. (See Section 46.)

- **Not this:** "There are four key drivers that are impacting our business."
- **But this:** "Four major/important trends/factors affect our business."
- **Or this (more personal):** "We can all see that there are four very strong forces/trends affecting our business."

Remember:

- Don't use euphemisms that people might reject (e.g., "downsize," "rightsize"). Speak straightforwardly about sensitive subjects.

- Don't be overly optimistic and let your rhetoric get too far ahead of the reality.

- Don't stretch the truth by hedging numbers (e.g., "in the neighborhood of," "as much as").

- Take credit for what you've actually done, but share the credit wherever appropriate.

- Be honest about your lack of experience or expertise in any particular area.

Consider emphasizing or highlighting your authenticity with such phrases as these:

- "I'm absolutely convinced that …."

- "The sum of my experience is that …."

- "One of my strongest beliefs is that …."

You'll discover many more ways to be authentic and show your best self. If you treat a speech first and foremost as an honest interaction between human beings, in which you are willing to show at least a little of your real self to the others, you'll become a better speaker. And it's more likely that your audience will feel better about having heard you—and be changed by what you say.

6. Be Clear About the "Audience Value" You're Presenting

Your listeners will be different (and perhaps even better) after they've heard you speak. But how? What are you trying to do? Seeking a change in thought or action? Presenting new information? Building unity around a particular commitment? At the beginning and the end of your speech, be specific about you want your listeners to do and always be sure they know *why* you're telling them what you're telling them. Here are a few examples.

Agenda:

- "These are our action items, our imperatives, for the months/years ahead. We can no more afford to ignore them than the matador can afford to ignore the bull."

Argument:

- "In the last few minutes, I've tried to show that ...." *[Recap key points.]*

Commitment:

- "Here is what I want each of you to do before you leave this room. I want each of you to make a silent, personal, *unshakable* commitment to *[goal]*.* Tell yourself that you *believe* in *[goal]*, that you *can [achieve goal]*, and that from this moment forth, you will *commit* yourself to *[goal]* and you will *commit* yourself to drawing upon all the talent and creativity in your organizations and in our industry and to taking the creative risks that will help you *[achieve goal]*. And then let us work and *[achieve goal] together*."
(***Note:*** The repetition of this word/phrase is intentional.)
- "I'll close by inviting you to join me/us in my/our commitment to ...."

Explanation/information:

- "I hope I've made it clear that …."
- "I hope it's clear, from all I've said, that …."
- "Among all the uncertainties, there are three certainties: …."

Immediate action:

- "Now is the time—and I call on all of *you*—to … *[whatever you want them to do]*."
- "So now I ask you to do three things:…."

Interpretation:

- *[At the beginning of a conference keynote speech:]* "In the next few minutes, I'd like to set up the rest of the day/week/etc. for you, so that when I'm done, you'll have a template that will help you interpret everything you hear—and apply it to your own particular activity."

Prediction/implications:

- "The changes I've talked about are unprecedented in magnitude. Those companies that understand and capitalize on such major changes—especially before their competitors—*always* emerge as big winners. What it all means for us is that …."
- "I've discussed the trends that are shaping our industry. What do they mean for us?"

Reaffirmation of basic principles:

- "Well, I doubt that I've broken any new ground or revealed any magic secrets to success. If anything, my experience has shown that the stratagies you've been hearing about for lo these many years—applied consistently and conscientiously—really do work."

Success:
- "Let me leave you with what I regard as the three keys to success in ...."

7. Create a Strong and Memorable Ending

The ending of your speech is a prime opportunity. People often remember what they've heard last.

End on a high and hopeful note. Express gratitude for the invitation and look forward to the future.

Make sure that in the last 30-60 seconds of your speech your listeners understand precisely what you're trying to tell them and what change in their thought or behavior you are advocating. Consider introducing your conclusion with a succinct summary of what you've said:

■ "My message to you tonight has been simple and straight-forward: ...." *[Give summary.]*

A very useful technique, which gives a sense of closure, is to return to your original theme and summarize it briefly:

■ "And that brings me back to my original theme ...." *[Give short recap of theme and its importance.]*

Here are some additional possibilities.

If you're talking about or urging the audience to embrace significant change, you may want to speak in terms of a reality check:

■ "Now, you [and your companies/organizations] are no doubt beginning to feel the opportunity—and the pressure—of all the changes I've been discussing. It's *how* we feel that pressure, *how* we view the changes, that makes all the difference. We have to act fast. We have to embrace—not avoid—change. And I use the word 'avoid' consciously, because I know there are companies [*or:* executives/individuals/etc.] that/who think that they can sort of pretend that this all isn't happening."

Urge the listeners to play an active role in determining their future; emphasize the importance of individual action and execution:

- "If we don't play an active role in deciding our destiny, it's a sure bet that others will do it for us."
- "To me, having ambitious goals and the means to reach them is truly inspiring. I hope you are as excited as I am about all the opportunities we have, opportunities to make a difference in this great organization/institution/industry. And now, *it is up to us. We* must make it happen."
- "There's so much more we can do. But it won't come automatically. We've got to be action-oriented and aggressive. We've got to go out and get it—together."

If the speech is a conference welcome or keynote, end by thanking the audience for attending and tell them what you hope they will gain from the conference:

- "I hope you find the *[length of conference]* to be informative, stimulating, and fun and that you'll come away with the plans and ideas and, most important, the excitement and enthusiasm that will make *[organization]* even stronger in the months and years ahead."
- "We hope that during the next *[length of conference]*, our conference will stimulate a new attitude, a new belief in yourselves and in our company, and a new orientation. These are the prerequisites for creating something remarkable—in fact, for successfully bringing about change of *any* kind, which is why I hope we can inspire them in *you*."
- "Again, welcome. I know you're going to enjoy the conference, and I wish you all the very best, in the next *[length of conference]* and throughout your careers. Thanks for being here."

To an organization:

- "I congratulate you on __ years of hard—and effective—work. And I wish you many more years of success."

If you've received an award from the organization:

- "I'm/We're proud to be associated with you—and very grateful for your recognition."

- "Let me close by thanking you once again for this honor … and wishing you a future that's even more successful than your past. Your mission is important, and I'm/we're proud to help you fulfill it."

Your very last phrases should be short and pithy, with an unmistakable sense of finality. Try to make the last sentence or two very simple rhythmically, with short, strong words, as in the examples below:

- "I'm looking forward to it with great enthusiasm. I hope you are too."

- [*After listing their challenges and tasks:*] "And as you do all that, I wish you every success and all the luck in the world!"

- [*After articulating goal:*] "And that is exactly what we must do."

- "You have embarked on a journey of [*whatever they're pursuing*]. The people around you, at your table, in this room, are your traveling companions, your colleagues, your friends. And so to all of you, I say, 'Good luck and bon voyage!'"

- "To me—and to a great many of us at [*company*] and all over the [*name of industry*] industry—the future has never been brighter. I hope you agree."

- "I ask you: with such abundant resources and talent, how can we go forward with anything but confidence and optimism that we *will* achieve our goal?"

- "You know, the pessimist complains about the wind, the

optimist expects it to change—but the realist adjusts the sails. Let *us* be realists. Let us adjust our sails and get ready for the next lap, because we are in this race to win!"

- "Thanks again for inviting me. I look forward to working with you, not only for our mutual success, but in the interests of *[higher cause]*."

- "Success is not a destination, but a journey. And I hope we'll make that journey together, with all the enthusiasm, commitment, and vision that have brought us this far. And whatever the future brings, I hope we'll be able to go on sharing successes for years and years to come."

- "*[Objective]* is a goal well worth pursuing, and I look forward to working with you to achieve it."

- "I predict that when we bring together all the elements— *[list topics you've discussed]*—we will create a critical mass and trigger a release of enthusiasm and creative energy that will unquestionably *[achieve desired goal]*."

- "I know that we *can [achieve goal]*. And I'm sure that we *will*."

- "Success is not assured, but one thing is—our destiny *is* in our hands."

- "So let's work together and get the job done."

- "Can we win? Can we *[achieve goal]*? I think that we can, we must, and we will."

- "And then, let us work and *[achieve goal] together*."

- "And now, *it is up to us. We* must make it happen."

- "Let's seize the opportunity and run with it."

- "It's simply a question of whether one has the desire and the commitment to do *everything* that's necessary, difficult as it may be. For if the desire and commitment are there, then everything else will follow."

- "Our task is to … *[goal]*. And that is a challenge that we welcome."

If you're speaking at or near the beginning of the year:

- "Thank you. I wish you all a successful 20__ and I hope it's a year of growth and prosperity … for *all* of us."

- "Already it's clear that 20__ is going to be an exciting year, a year of growth and positive changes for all of us. So let me offer you my best wishes … for *your* best year *ever*."

To business partners:

- "All of us at *[company/organization]* look forward to working more closely with you, as our industry enters a new era of great promise and exciting opportunity."

To a group of public relations or government affairs professionals:

- "Finally, I would leave you with these words from Emily Dickinson:'Truth is such a rare thing it is delightful to tell it.' Your mission, difficult as it is, is to tell the truth, nothing more and nothing less, and as you go about it, I wish you all the luck and success in the world."

8. If There Will Be a Q&A Session After Your Speech

Early in the speech, set up your Q&A:

- "Later on, I'll be interested in hearing your comments and I'll be pleased to try to answer your questions."

At the end, lead into your Q&A:

- "Thank you again for inviting me. I hope that what I've said has prompted some questions, so let's get to them!"
- "Thank you very much for this opportunity to speak with you. I would now be pleased to hear any questions you may have."
- "Thank you again for inviting me today. And now let's get to the comments and questions!"
- "Thanks for your attention—and now let's open it up for your questions and comments."

Part Two

Speeches at Internal Meetings and Conferences

The most important fact about these speeches is what the listeners have in common—their relationship to their organization and, secondarily, to their group, business unit, or profession.

9. General Employee or Management Briefings

"State of the business" and strategy overview speeches usually consist of a discussion of the organization's performance, followed by comments on the outlook for the next year, quarter, etc. But the key to making these speeches effective is to understand the audience's perspective, which, compared with that of the senior executive, is quite narrow and usually limited to a particular plant, function, or office. It's essential to familiarize your listeners with the big picture, but without a lot of mind-numbing detail.

You can organize the speech around the standard dimensions of the strategic plan: competitive environment, the needs of your customers, the activities of your competitors, and distinctive strengths and competencies the company can use to accelerate its growth and achieve its business objectives. Follow that with a description of the various strategic thrusts that, together with its strengths, will make your company more successful than its peers and lead to real, sustainable growth.

If potentially disruptive changes—layoffs, divestitures— are under way, the listeners need reassurance and a sense of where it's all leading. They want to know that management has a handle on the problems and really knows what to do to grow the business. And they want to hear what they can do to help.

Aim for a macro view that will help people outside headquarters to understand what's going on.

In addition to the content and organization of your speech, one or more of the following strategies may help you connect with your audience and achieve your purpose.

(Also see Section 44 for specific advice on communicating with employees.)

Begin with a Note of Enthusiasm and Organizational Unity

- "Today I want to talk about what's going on at *[company/organization]*, what's hot, what's working, what we're excited about as we [wind up the year and head into 20__ *or whatever time-setting expression is appropriate*]. I think you're going to find it exciting too, because these are the innovative, business-building initiatives that *your* work is supporting."

- "It's great to have this opportunity to bring you up to speed on how the business is doing."

- "We all need to do our part [to turn the business around *or whatever the goal is*]. This is not a headquarters issue or a sales issue or a manufacturing/etc. issue. We *all* own the results and we need to work together to build the business."

Review the Strategies and Connect Employees' Jobs with the Corporate Plan

- "You should never change a winning strategy ... and we have not just one but *[number of strategies]* that have brought us this far ... and we're going to stick with them. Let me recap them for you, just to make sure we're all on the same page ... and to remind you that each of the many diverse programs and projects you've executed so flawlessly is simply an expression of one of *[number of strategies]* basic themes."

- "I want to give you a sense of what's happening all over the company and show you how what's going on in your office, in your plant, or in your staff function is all part of a bigger and very important story of teamwork and success *[or whatever the corporate values are]*."

If Your Organization Is Playing Catch-up

■ "Can we *[again]* attain *[specific competitive position]*? Yes. But to do it, we'll need the same intensity, the same single-minded determination that we see among our competitors, foreign and domestic."

■ "Unless we want to play a perpetual game of catch-up, we have to do more than just meet our competitors on a day-to-day basis. We have to anticipate their moves. We have to understand their ultimate strategies—and then out-strategize them and outsmart them."

If Appropriate, Congratulate Them for Their Cost-Containment Efforts

■ "What you've done on costs—despite increasing pressure—has not only made significant contributions to the bottom line. It's enabled us to be aggressive, *progressive*, and adept in the marketplace."

■ "I think you've done a *great* job. But I know that there's more waste and inefficiency that we can root out. I know we can improve processes, clarify roles, and find smarter ways to do things. I always know we can do better."

Note That Continuous Competitive Pressure Is a Given, as Is Continuous Improvement

■ "I remember seeing a Nike ad with the slogan, 'There is no finish line.' And it reminded me of the way things are in business too. There is no finish line. The competition never goes away, and we're always looking for ways to do better and raise our game."

If the Entire Industry Is Struggling, You Can Note That Fact and Make a Motivational Point

- "Now, it's true that some of our competitors are hurting as well, and for many of the same reasons. But that's no reason for us to be complacent. There's little comfort in being fellow passengers on the sinking Titanic, right? We want to be on the lifeboats. We want to survive. And more—we want to win."

Note That Productivity Savings Alone Are Not Sufficient to Grow the Bottom Line

- "Our long-term success will depend on how well we add consumer value to our products/services; that's what generates *real* growth. We can't rely on productivity to make our numbers. The purpose of productivity savings is to make the dollars available to reinvest in the business—and our ability to do *that* is what will make the numbers."

Show That You Appreciate the Difficulty of Their Jobs and Their Challenges as Managers

- "You're constantly forced to make tough decisions, like *[examples of decisions]*. And through it all, the competition is out there, snapping at your heels like an ugly pit bull."

Articulate the Fundamental Balancing Act of Management

- "What it all comes down to is that we have to approach our business with the proper balance of analysis and action, of preparation and implementation, of caution and quickness."
- "The nimble organization [which is what we need to be] is like a jazz combo. Now, I don't know much about jazz, but I do know that the musicians are actually composing in real

time, yet somehow they're all at the same point in the song. That's an excellent model for our business: we all adhere to an agreed-upon strategy and go forward together—but there's lots of room for improvising the execution to take advantage of changing conditions. So that's the key: coordinated strategies ... with freedom of execution."

Emphasize the Need for Constant Re-examination and Renewal

■ "We need to be looking critically at everything we do. Long-established practices, procedures, and habits of mind are the most suspect. According to an old Japanese proverb, 'If you sit on a stone for three years, you will get used to it.' What stones are *we* sitting on? What have *we* gotten used to? Even worse, a company can go into decline not only by continuing to do old, familiar things, but by continuing to do the *very* things that made it successful! It's happened many times, to some of the greatest companies—GM, and Sears, to name just two. Companies like Admiral, Philco, Singer Sewing Machines, Royal, and Underwood used to be household names. Where are they now?"

Summarize the Basic Structure of Your Presentation

■ "Well, there you have a quick overview of the business, plus some thoughts on how we got to where we are and where we need to go."

■ "Today I've talked about our financial results, and—even more important—I've identified some areas where we can capitalize on our size and skills to win—for all of our stakeholders, including our customers, our consumers, and our shareholders."

End on an Optimistic and Inspirational Note

- "I once read a comment by Phil Jackson: 'This game is about 80% energy and confidence and about 20% tactical stuff. If you have the energy and become the aggressors, that really bodes well for a team.' What's true in basketball is true in management, now more than ever. Both games are fluid and dynamic. You do have a game plan, but still, you can't use preset plays for every occasion. You've got to continually improvise, respond quickly, and anticipate changes. When each team has nearly equal talent and resources, then it's attitude, energy, confidence, and intensity that define the winner. We already have the talent and resources. So let's make sure *we* have the attitude—the confidence—of a winner."

- *[If appropriate:]* "Now we're starting to put it all together. We've had a taste of success, and I have a feeling that it's made us hungry for more. I want to thank you, because with your support, we've gone a long way very quickly. And I have no doubt that we're going to show everybody that our best days are still ahead."

- "I know we're up to the challenge. And ____ months from now, hard as it is to believe on this beautiful spring/summer day, we'll be looking out at snowdrifts, looking forward to another joyous holiday season, and looking back at another very successful year for our company/organization."

10. Gatherings of a Particular Management Level or Functional Specialty

Most of the themes and phrases in Section 9 apply to this type of speech as well. In addition, you may want to do one or more of the following.

In Speeches to a Particular Staff Group, Reassure the Audience of Their Value and Bright Future

- "Career and professional success are within your grasp. You already have what you need: a commitment to continued immersion in the real content of the business ... plus an awareness of *your* special tools, techniques, and perspectives. The more you use those tools to help shape and direct and grow our business, the more you'll ensure your professional success—and enrich/increase your value to our company/organization."

If Appropriate, Point Out What an Efficient Organization They Are

- "*[Name of staff/organization]* is actually one very lean team[—and that's not a reference to their weight, although they are pretty trim folks, probably because they work so hard]." *[Follow with example(s) of how much they've been able to do.]*

Make a Suggestion for Ongoing Professional and Personal Growth

- "I have a simple piece of advice: become the person you would like to promote. Continually ask yourself what you would look for in such a person. Intelligence, dedication, hard work—certainly. But also honesty, integrity, sensitivity to the needs of other people, the willingness to *give* to other people—qualities not only of the good manager, but of the good *life* as well. Set your own list of personal goals, just as you set goals for your business unit. And work conscientiously to meet them."

■ "We got to where we are by continuous, proactive self-development—by taking control of our careers. But we can't stop here. We should all be identifying our own skills gaps, getting feedback from new sources, and making ourselves available for task forces or assignments that help us grow. We not only help ourselves, we also set a powerful example for our people, because when they see that senior managers are still pursuing self-development, they'll be motivated to do the same."

Distinguish Problems from Opportunities

■ "Peter Drucker's advice is 'Don't solve problems. Pursue opportunities.' And that's my mindset, too. If you see things in terms of problems, it's all too easy to go for the quick fix. But try to see opportunities, and you'll discover strategies that lead to basic changes in the way you do business. And that's when you really get at the root causes of the so-called 'problems.'"

■ "I sincerely believe that change, along with all the uncertainty and discomfort, really does bring this opportunity. What we do about today's challenges will, in large measure, determine what tomorrow brings. Our task is not to accept change passively, but to lead it—and to manage it creatively. For the health of our business enterprises, for the good of the society we serve, and the fortunes of those who follow us, we really can do no less."

Affirm the Importance of the Function/Profession to the Organization's Success

- "There's a tremendous opportunity for *[function/profession]* in our company today. *You* will be the ones that senior management depends on to *[whatever their strategic role is]*. It's another way—and a very significant way—for you to be true strategic partners."

- "Good morning/afternoon/evening. Let me say right off that I am absolutely delighted to be here with the finest, smartest, most competent *[if audience is involved in any competitive activity, such as sales or law, consider adding* and winningest*]* bunch of *[whatever their specialty is]* in the industry … and perhaps *in the entire country*. All of us at *[company]* are pleased and proud that you're on our team."

- "To us in senior management, you are key business partners. You share our risk, our responsibility, and our rewards. You have numerous and influential roles to play. And we're counting on you to play them to the best of your extraordinary abilities—because we've never needed them more."

To a science/research group:

- "We look to you to be innovators and agents of change. We need you to help us grow our business by satisfying our consumers—and then going beyond satisfaction, to surprise and delight them by giving them what they didn't even *know* they wanted. And we need you to help us stand out from the competition, with *[whatever your competitive product/service advantages are]*."

- "You should be proud to be playing such a strategic role, proud that you're doing so many significant things to help our company/organization achieve its goals [*or:* its goal of *(describe goal)*]."

To marketing or other creative people:

- "To grow the business, we have to respond to—and ideally, anticipate—customer needs with superior products/services. That process begins with you. Your creativity is at the very foundation of our success."

- "I have the greatest respect for your talents, because I know how exceptional the true innovator really is—and how fortunate our company is to have so many creative people to help us *[fulfill your mission or strategic goals—specify them]*."

Urge the Audience to Pursue Continuous Self-Development

- All of you got to where you are by virtue of serious self-development—but don't stop here. Seek out instruction in areas where you need development. Get feedback from new sources. Be available for task forces or assignments that help you grow. In Zen Buddhism, there's the notion of the 'beginner's mind'—something that's very helpful to adopt every now and then. You simply take the position that you don't know anything and that you have everything to learn. When your people see that the leaders of the organization are still developing themselves, it's going to have a huge impact on the way they see their own self-development. It shows them they have the opportunity to grow and develop over a long career—and it gives them the motivation to do so."

If You're Speaking at a Conference, Urge the Audience to Network, Build Relationships, and Have Fun

- "I've always found that things are so much easier when you know the person on the other end, as opposed to trading faxes with a name and an office. So I hope this conference will help you develop personal relationships and open up new opportunities to share knowledge. Because it's a simple fact of life: when everybody's so busy, you're more willing to go out of your way to help people you know."

- "I hope you'll take advantage of the many opportunities for networking—not just 'Hi, what's your name?' but the building of solid relationships that will enable you to exchange ideas more regularly and to benefit from each other's experience and expertise, not only now, but in the future as well."

- "I hope you'll have some fun—and not just from the recreational activities we've planned. Meeting new people and playing with new ideas is also fun, as anyone under the age of 10 will tell you, and I hope you can enjoy yourselves in that way, too."

Urge the Audience to Develop a Tolerance for Ambiguity and for Multiple Points of View

- "Constantly immerse yourself in new information. Tolerate—even welcome—ambiguity. Be a fountainhead of diverse points of view. Put your ego aside and search— always impatiently—for the best answer. Because when you do all of that, the quality of your thought processes will be a model and an inspiration for everyone around you."

If They're Struggling with a Serious Issue, Assure Them of Senior Management's Support

- "I also want to assure you of senior management's support. We're very much aware of the importance of [whatever issue they're struggling with] to our business/organization, and we're ready to help you in any way we can."

If the Audience Will Be a Significant Help in Implementing the Plans You've Laid Out

■ "I know that you can—and will—play a leadership role in these initiatives. And I know that you can—and will—be instrumental as we achieve our goals and objectives in 20___ and beyond."

End by Complimenting the Audience

■ "I'll wind up where I began: by telling you once again what a great group you are and how proud I am to be associated with you. *[Consider adding* And with winners like you on our team, I'm convinced that the best is yet to come!*]*"

■ "I hope it's clear, from what I've been saying, that your contribution to the success of our company is both significant and growing ... and that in the years ahead, we'll need—more than ever—your special skills and your unique perspective on our business."

11. Announcing New Strategy, Vision, or Direction (Including Reorganizations and Mergers/Acquisitions)

The content of this speech will largely be dictated by internal forces, just as the event itself is shaped by external forces. Nevertheless, you have some opportunities to put your individual stamp on the content of the speech, to personalize its language, and to use whatever techniques are most natural to you (including the ones below) in order to build enthusiasm and support.

If the changes are coming in a strictly top-down manner, I advise you not to overdo the enthusiasm. Employees will pretty much go along with anything, because they have no choice. However, if lower-level people and/or task forces have actually had input, emphasize this fact. The general buy-in will then be somewhat more genuine.

Aside from the details of the new strategy, your speech might do one or more of the following.

Emphasize the Need to Initiate Change

- "I hope it's clear that, over time, the way we do business would very likely disadvantage us even if our world were standing still. But it isn't. It's changing—and fast."
- "To be successful in our/this environment, indeed to survive, we must *create* the change that leads to distinct competitive advantage."
- "In an environment like ours, where standing still means drifting backward, there's no choice but to go ahead."

If Appropriate, Talk in Terms of a Course Correction and Leadership

- "Course correction is inevitable when you're navigating in unexplored places. When you're a path-breaker, there is by definition no map, so you have to create one as you go. And sometimes the map you draw is slightly off, so you need to revise it. But I would argue that it is *far* better to be out front, leading the way, than to be in the rear, trying to get started."

If Appropriate, Give the Audience Some Sense of the Scope and Importance of the Changes

- "Today is one of the most important days in the history of our company. And I am *so* proud to share it with all of you, who have done so much to make *[company]* the extraordinary company it is today. *Your* talent, creativity, and hard work have helped us come this far … and that's why it's so appropriate to have all of you here, as we begin to take the *next* giant step in the evolution of *[name of company]*."

If the Strategy Is Designed to Retain Customers, Emphasize the Importance of This Goal

- "A customer is a precious commodity; it cost us a great deal of time, effort, and expense to earn his or her loyalty, his or her 'custom' or habit, and—a very important fact— the cost of keeping that customer is much lower than that of gaining a new customer, which is why we simply cannot tolerate losing customers to a competitor."

Urge the Audience to Become Excited About the Coming Changes

- "There are two kinds of excitement. One is the kind you feel when somebody with a knife in his hand is chasing you down an alley. The other comes when you hit a home run or sink a hole in one. Too often it's only the prospect of bad times that gives us this emotion. We need to get excited about making good things happen."

Emphasize the Importance of All the Preparation That's Been Done

- "There's a wonderful Danish proverb that says, 'He who would leap high must take a long run.' We've been building the momentum for a very great leap. And the sooner we start our run, the better."

Emphasize Personal Responsibility for the Future

- "A great historian[1] once wrote [—and all of you who are sailors know this, I'm sure—], 'the winds and waves are always on the side of the ablest navigators.' As we chart the future of our business, we have to be the ablest navigators of all. And while the outcome may be in doubt, the goals have never been clearer."

Acknowledge the Challenges

- "What it all comes down to is that in a business that has rarely known a dull moment, we're heading for some of the most challenging and exciting times we've ever known."

- "There's a famous quote [from the Roman philosopher Horace, (65-68 BCE)] that 'adversity reveals genius and prosperity conceals it.' And it's true: our business is being tested in the fires of competition hotter than any we've ever known. And I believe that were coming out of them tougher and more resourceful than we've ever been."

1. Edward Gibbon, *History of the Decline and Fall of the Roman Empire*, Chapter LXVIII.

■ "I'm fully aware that what I've laid out for you today is a highly ambitious agenda—*[recap]*. Can we do it all? Well, I look at what we've got going for us, and I'm convinced that we can." *[From here, you can transition to a discussion of the company's strengths.]*

Emphasize the Timeliness or Boldness of the New Strategy

■ "Here's a great quote I got from the VP of a high-tech company:[2] 'By the time the rules of the game are clear, the windows of opportunity are closed.' I like that—and I would add this: 'But when you *make* the rules, you *create* the window.'"

Make a Personal Commitment; Ask the Audience to Join You in It

■ "I intend to pursue our strategy them with the best I have in me … and I urge each of you to do the same, so that the coming years will see a company that's even stronger, more vibrant, and prouder than it is today."

Urge the Audience to Break with the Past; Charge Them with Successful Execution

■ "We have an opportunity to 'repaint the canvas'—to rearrange our reality according to the vision we've set for ourselves, to make fundamental changes in ourselves and the way we do business. It's all about having the courage to break with the past to create something new and better. Miles Davis, the great jazz musician, did that—several times. So did Pablo Picasso: you look at paintings from different periods in his life and it's hard to believe they were all done

2. Santhanam "Slim" Shekar, VP, Business and Policy Group, SRI International.

50

by the same person. And those are just the examples that *I* can think of. Many other great artists were not content to do the same thing throughout their careers, even if they got better and better at it [*even if it was working for them*]. You can do the same. We've given you the tools. We've provided the design, the strategy, the vision. Now it's up to you. *You* must go ahead and get the job done."

- "The prospect of big changes may make us apprehensive, but I think we have to remember that even if you *are* on the right track, you'll get run over if you just sit there. Well, we *are* on the right track. *[Consider adding* And we've come too far to get run over now. We need to pull ahead. And that means having the courage to change ... and to dare to be different.*]*"

- "Does all of this sound bold, even outrageous, to you? I hope so! I once saw a quote that pretty much sums it up for me: 'The people who are crazy enough to think they can change the world ... are often the ones who do.'"

- "So, if we have to do things in a different way, well, we'll do them in a different way. And we'll have to face up to whatever that means. And we *will* face up to it, as honestly and as best we can."

Put the Merger/Acquisition in the Context of the Organization's Strategy

- "It just doesn't pay to internally develop a business that is not closely related to our current activities or does not have a strong strategic justification. That's why, in areas that demand major new assets or knowledge of consumers/ clients/end users, we consider acquisition."

12. Urging Support of a Political Action Committee

Your specific points and arguments will, of course, be governed by the organization's political position and issues. Here are some general themes.

Explain That Much of What the Company Does Is Controlled by Government Policy

- "Why do we have to get involved in politics? After all, you and I come to work each day, we try to do a great job, and we expect that if everyone else does too, we'll be successful. Simple, right? Wrong. It takes more than that. Every day, in Washington, D.C., and in state governments all over our country, legislators and regulators are making decisions that affect the way we do business."

Note That the Health of the Business Requires a Certain Political/Regulatory Environment

- "Government at all levels has a lot to say about our company's taxes, investments, and other financial affairs. Of course, once these decisions are made, we have to abide by them. And that's why we've got to have a voice in *how* they're made. We need to be politically well informed and politically active."
- "In *every* session of Congress, measures are proposed that could have a significant impact on our bottom line."
  [Optional: mention specific laws and regulations.]
- *[If true (otherwise, modify as necessary):]* "There is virtually no activity in our business that does not, in some way, at some time, come under governmental oversight."

Note the Growing Strength of Special-Interest Groups

■ "As the political and social issues that affect our business become more intense and complex, special-interest groups, with their own access to the political process, are getting better and better organized—and more and more influential."

Use a Cost-Savings Analogy to Take a Businesslike Approach to the PAC

■ "If you could identify an area of your operations where you could save the company a million dollars in costs … or even $10 million …, would you put a plan in place to do so? Of course you would—it's a no-brainer! Well, the political issues facing us have a very real impact on our costs."

Explain That a PAC Is a Way to Help Elect Politicians Who Support the Organization's Views: It's a Requirement for Business Success

■ "There *are* candidates who share our concerns and who agree with us on how we can most effectively serve our consumers and the public interest. But we need to know who they are. We need to get access to them. And we need to support them."

■ "With support from our PAC, candidates who support our interests can communicate more effectively with voters, so they're more likely to get elected."

■ "A PAC is a powerful way to get access to politicians, thus a voice in the decisions that affect us, virtually everywhere in our business."

■ "A PAC is not just about money. It's a defense of our right to protect and grow our business and to ensure the livelihoods of all *[company]* people."

- "What kind of representatives do we want in power? Those who will listen to our arguments with an open mind and who will be interested in creating and keeping jobs in our industry." *[Add criteria as appropriate.]*
- "It's critically important to help elect legislators who share our perspectives on the issues that matter to us. Our PAC is the only campaign-funding mechanism that enables us to go head-to-head with our opponents on those issues."

Speak in Terms of Strength in Numbers

- "Our PAC will unite you with hundreds/thousands of your fellow *[company]* people in a common political cause. It will amplify your voice many times over. It will make sure that politicians hear our message."
- "When you join a PAC, you have more clout than you could as a individual. You can reach more candidates/politicians than you could on your own."
- "A PAC is a strategic way to mobilize our people, who are truly an underutilized resource in this area."

Make a Statement About Government Intrusion

- "Are we going to head in the direction of more regulation, more bureaucracy, more intrusion in our personal and professional lives? Or are we going to make progress toward a leaner, more efficient government that is committed to individual freedom?"

At a Solicitation Meeting, Close the Deal

- "So, if we care about the future of our industry, of our company, and of our own livelihoods, none of us will leave this room without pledging a donation. However you choose to do it, please give, so that we can continue to go to Washington and fight for an environment in which our business can grow and be successful."

13. Visit to a Manufacturing Plant

The content of your speech will probably be some sort of a report from the corporate level, so the advice in Section 9 applies to this type of speech. (I'm assuming no problems with labor contracts, plant closings, etc.)

Before the visit, get information on plant personnel and on recent individual and plant achievements. Then, in your speech, express your appreciation for the individual contributors. Consider leading off with "When they asked Yogi Berra what makes a great manager, his answer was simple: 'A great team.'"

If You Have Operating Experience, Show Your Firsthand Understanding of the Complexity of Manufacturing a Quality Product

- "Those of you who know me know that I am fascinated by the complexity of manufacturing—and I have the greatest of respect for people who actually make the product. I've always been tremendously interested in both the manufacturing process and the product itself. And I love to stay current on new products ... and on the technology that improves both the process and the product."

Express Management Commitment

- "I give you my commitment that we will be open to creative suggestions—to *any* sincere, constructive answers to the question, 'What can top management do to help you reach *[whatever the overarching goal is]*?'"

Part Three

Speeches to External Organizations

A s with internal speeches, the most important fact about speeches to external organizations is whatever the audience has in common—what brings them together as an organization. To prepare for these speeches, you—or your PR person or agency—should gather as much information as possible about your listeners and the topic they would like you to speak about.

This part contains general areas you might want to address along with the assigned topic. An added convenience, I've put the various examples of phrase types in the approximate order in which they might occur in a speech.

14. Some Possibilities for the Opening[1]

Find out if there are any government officials or other dignitaries you need to recognize at the outset.

Praise the importance of face-to-face contact with this particular audience:

- "It really is a pleasure—and a great opportunity—for me to be face-to-face with so many leaders of the *[name of industry]* industry and to share with you some of my thoughts on where our industry is going."

- "Thank you and good afternoon/morning/evening. I'm honored to have been invited to address this distinguished group of leaders."

Consider making complimentary reference to the organization's founder, motto, longevity, and/or values. Say just enough to show that you understand them, but not too much to be patronizing.

If the organization is celebrating a major anniversary:

- "I'm both pleased and proud to have the opportunity to address an organization that celebrating its 25th *[or whichever]* year of *[whatever the organization does]*. I wish you another 25 *[or whichever]* years and more of progress and service. And I'm confident that my wish will come true. I believe that you have a great future."

- "As you begin your ___ decade, I offer you my very best wishes for many more years of progress, service, and success in fulfilling your remarkable mission [of …] *[summarize the mission, if appropriate]*."

1. For specific speech-opening devices and strategies, see my book, *Writing Great Speeches: Professional Techniques You Can Use* (Allyn & Bacon, 1997).

Since external audiences will probably have spent extra time and energy to attend your presentation, you might thank them for the effort and, if appropriate, for braving any inclement weather. You can say that many organizations simply wouldn't exist without people taking time to meet face to face or "as Woody Allen said, 'showing up is 80% of life.'" Then add something like "I believe it. There's no substitute for human contact."

If appropriate, congratulate the organization on its growth. This one will require a little research and mathematical calculation.

Example:

- "The dramatic growth of this conference is proof of how successful you've been. Your first conference, in *[year]*, was attended by about ___ people. This year you have ___ attendees. Pretty impressive numbers! Actually, I'm a little envious. I'd love to be able to say that we've grown our business by ___% in ___ years."

If Your Assigned Topic Is Broad or Bland, Try to Take a Fresh Perspective on It:

- "My purpose here today to take a good hard look at, reevaluate, reinterpret, maybe even rediscover, in a sense, something that we've thought and talked about for quite a long time: *[whatever the topic is]*."

If You're Speaking to a Group Whose Profession or Expertise Is Somewhat Different from Your Own:

- "Of course, I'm an outsider whose knowledge of your world can hardly touch your own. But, as James Thurber once said, 'It is better to know some of the questions than all the answers.'"

If the Locale Has Been "Home" to You in Some Way

■ "There are many definitions of 'home': home is where you grew up; home is where you live; home is where the heart is; home is where the mortgage is; home is where, when you go there, they have to take you in. But when I use the word 'home' about *[city]*, I have something different—and very specific—in mind. *[City]* is truly one of my 'homes,' because of the many years I've spent here, the many projects I've been involved in, both business and civic, and the many strong friendships that came out of it all and that are still a part of my life *[or other details that make it home to you].* "

At the End, Thank Them Again for Coming:

■ "Again, let me say how pleased I am that you came today/tonight. You've been a wonderful audience, and I hope you've enjoyed the day/evening as much as I have."

If the Organization Is Embarking on a New Program or Project:

■ "I offer you my best wishes for success in this extraordinary mission. Go to it! And best of luck to you all!

15. Service or Civic Organization

These organizations would include Rotary, the National Business League, Boy Scouts and Girl Scouts, the Chamber of Commerce, etc. What all of these audiences have in common is, at least in part, is interest in and knowledge about business. They're also interested in current events and new knowledge.

If you're a member of the organization that's invited you, make some reference to your relationship, experience, or familiarity with it. If you're not a member, familiarize yourself with the organization and, in your introduction, speak highly of its strengths, values, and contributions. Don't overdo it; less is more. Make the audience feel good about who they are and what they do. Then transition into your main theme.

Praise the Audience

- "It's an honor and pleasure to be here among so many [future] economists and business leaders and, just as important, among so many people who really understand economics and the free enterprise system."
- "As Peter Drucker once observed, 'Whenever you see a successful business, someone once made a courageous decision.' I see a lot of courageous decisions represented here in this room, and I congratulate you for them, wherever and whenever they were made."

If You're Speaking at an Anniversary Event or the Organization Is in an Anniversary Year, Congratulate the Audience and Offer Best Wishes

- "I'd like to offer my warmest congratulations to [organiza-

tion] on its *[number]* anniversary … and also my best
wishes for another *[same/larger number]* years of fine and
loyal service to this community."

■ "Let me be among the first to congratulate *[organization]*
on its ___ years of business/industry leadership."

Identify the Challenges That All Companies Face, Regardless of Size

■ "All of us here are concerned with business success. And it
may seem like something of a paradox, but it's true: the
big, obvious differences between my company and yours
are actually the superficial ones. Down where it really
counts—at the level of individual performance and product quality—we all face the same problems; we all have
the same goals."

Identify with the Organization's Values

■ *[Rotary example:]* "I feel right at home here, because of your
Rotarian ideals of professionalism, fellowship, and service—all of which are very familiar to me and high on my
list of values to be preached and practiced."

If You're Speaking to a Business or Service Group That Has Helped Revitalize the Local Economy

■ "Thank you, good afternoon, and congratulations to each
and every one of you. Now, I know it's a little unusual to
start off a speech by congratulating the audience, but in
this case, it's really appropriate. You see, it's you—the business community of *[city]* and everyone you've been able to
capitalize and motivate and energize—who have defied all
the naysayers and brought this city/region back to economic health and prosperity."

■ "This is one city/state/region that's learned that change is the only thing that's permanent. You've learned to live with it, to like it, and to make a success of it."

Discuss the Wider Social Impact of Business

- "Your companies and mine create jobs and business opportunities that strengthen the economies of the countries in which we do business. Together, we can help improve the quality of people's lives—people by the hundreds of millions—people on every continent of our planet. If we fulfill all these higher obligations of leadership, we will have done more than provide products and jobs. We will have left a strong and lasting heritage—of healthy business enterprises, creative innovation, and economic stability and growth. Truly, those who follow us deserve nothing less than that."

Refer to the Social Obligations of Business

- "America is the land of eternal optimism; we believe that the future can improve upon the past—but only if we face the challenges of the present. And by 'we' I mean our whole society: government, schools, labor, social service groups, volunteers—and corporations."

- *[Continue from point above or use separately:]* "We in business owe the world more than quality products and services at fair prices. Critical issues—like _____—affect the society of which we are a part, so they affect us as well. It's our responsibility to help make a difference."

16. Business Forum/Local Economic Club

All of the advice in the Section 15 applies to speeches to these audiences. In addition, these are the kinds of audiences who would be receptive to a pro-capitalist position. For instance, you might urge the various businesses and industries to work together to oppose detrimental environmental regulation:

■ "Any differences between us are far less important than the *freedom* for all of us to build and run successful businesses in an environmentally and socially responsible way."

17. Professional/Intellectual Forums

Speeches to such groups as Town Hall of California and regional or local World Affairs Councils are essentially the same as those discussed in Section 14. In addition, consider praising the organization in a way that's commensurate with its eminence. For example:

- "It's a real pleasure to be here at one of the most eminent and prestigious business forums in the country."

18. Commencement Speeches

These are the world's most ridiculed speeches and, if only for a short time, the most visible ones as well. The best you can do, given the situation (an uncomfortable, impatient audience waiting to party) and the tradition (legions of commencement speakers who have preceded you), is to be as personal and as focused on the audience as possible, thus increasing your chances of saying something interesting, even memorable.

A commencement speech is for the graduates. It should honor, inspire, inform, and entertain them. Beyond that, there's really no requirement—other than brevity. The subject matter is wide open.

Types of Commencement Speeches

Most commencement speeches fall into one of the following categories.

"My Favorite Subject" Speech. This one is appropriate mainly for the heaviest hitters—people who are such well-known experts that whatever they say on their subject will be worth hearing. It's also OK for very eminent alumni.

"The World Out There" Speech. This is an account of the world that the graduates are entering, from the perspective of the speaker, often including advice as to how they can prepare for it or opinions on how their education has prepared them for it—if only they know how to use it properly. The problem here is to avoid the obvious. Don't tell them things about the world that they know from watching TV or surfing the Net. This speech can be edgy. (See below.)

"You Can Make a Difference" Speech. This is a variation on "the world out there." Make clear to them what their potential is and argue that, despite the complexity and demands of life, they can and should keep their aspirations high. The pitfall here is windiness. The remedy is to be specific: you must argue convincingly that they indeed can make a difference and you must offer specific suggestions for doing so.

"What's Wrong with the World?" (or "Single Issue") **Speech.** This is another variation on "the world out there." The focus here is on some personal trait, some aspect of human nature that's at the root of many of our problems. The problem here is to avoid being trite: most of our sins are well-known. But if, in your experience, there's one thing that stands out, that's more harmful than almost everything else, then the speech can be convincing and authentic. A subcategory: "The solution is at hand and our task is to recognize and apply it."

"The Point of It All" Speech. This one focuses on the education they've just completed and addresses the question of what it all means. It's particularly appropriate for institutions that are proud of their curriculum or of some aspect of it. But you must be well acquainted with the institution, in order to avoid irrelevancy. (A subcategory: how education and experience complement each other.)

"Enduring Values" Speech. This is the classic "advice to graduates" speech. Focus on principles of thought and behavior that transcend time and make success more likely. If you choose this theme, you risk sounding pompous, which is why the best approach to this speech (unless you are a renowned philosopher) is lightweight, with advice that is wry or even humorous—but nevertheless substantive.

"Edgy" Speech. This one is a risk, but if you have strong opinions, solid expertise, and a valid argument, you can pull it off. Take a point of view that's not mainstream, even controversial. Or tell graduates hard truths about adult life. But don't make it a downer; be wry and inspiring. Edginess, done well, always holds audiences.

"What I've Learned" Speech. Graduates are "works in progress." Your maturity and your personal view of what "adulthood" means can be of value to them. This one draws extensively on personal experience. The pitfall: too much "I/me" focus. The remedies: use self-deprecating humor to illustrate your points and make specific connections between your experience and the graduates' personal development and growth.

Whichever way you decide to go, here are some general suggestions.

Address and Greet Everyone Graciously
- "*[Name(s) of individual(s)*, e.g., the institution's president*]*, trustees, parents, faculty, and, of course, all of you in the Class of 20__, my warmest congratulations!"

Compliment the Audience
- "Thank you and good morning/afternoon/evening! *[Name(s) of dean and/or president of institution]*, faculty, graduates of the Class of 20__, distinguished guests, and family and friends of the graduates, it's an honor and pleasure to share this morning/day/evening with you. I extend my warmest congratulations and most sincere best wishes to all of the graduates whose hard work and success has earned them the privilege of being here today."

To the graduates:
- "It's taken a lot of work, hope, and commitment to bring you all to this very special day, and I want you to know what a pleasure it is to be here and share it with you."

To the family members:
- "Your graduate's success is partly yours. It reflects your support and contributions—both financial and emotional. So now let me recognize, acknowledge, and congratulate all of the graduates' families for all you've done to make this day possible and memorable for your graduate."

Comment on the Skills That the Graduates Have Acquired
Example:

- "You've learned how to absorb, organize, and analyze new information. You've learned to respect—and even reconcile—opposing points of view. In a nutshell, you've learned how to *think*. That's just as important as the actual content of your training—more important, even, because life is changing and growing so rapidly. So I hope your college/university experience will continue to benefit you, long after you've forgotten the specific facts that got you through your final exams."

Urge Students to Be Creative in Seeking Opportunities for Service

- "One of the advantages of today's constant and rapid social and technological change is unexpected new opportunities for service. Sometimes the opportunities come in the form of social problems—homelessness, illiteracy, job displacement, the need for day and health care—that either are totally new or take different forms.

Sometimes the opportunities come in the form of new trends, movements, organizations that need people or support. Be on the lookout for them. Stay aware and well-informed, because you're bound to hit on something that matches your talents and concerns."

Emphasize the Importance of Cultivating a Good Reputation Through Doing Good

■ "Socrates said that you should 'regard your good name as the richest jewel you can possess,' and he added, 'the way to gain a good reputation is to endeavor to be what you desire to appear.' Put simply: if we want to look good, we must *be* good … and *do* good. There's great power in having a reputation that reflects who you are and what you stand for."

To Lead into an "Advice to Graduates" Speech

■ "To those of you who are about to enter the world of work, I thought I might do my bit to 'top off' your college education and help you get ready for that world you're entering, by offering some preparatory training—sort of a 'Cliff's Notes' on that thick and complicated book called 'Life.'"

Talk About How Students Must Build on Their Education

■ "I hope that your education here at *[institution]* has helped you think about what it means to really live the good life. You now decide for yourselves, as you start to plan your life … and as you deal with the unplanned events that life invariably foists upon you. It's like learning to drive with the manual in your hand. And once you make the wrong choices, it's too late. So now you must take the education and intellectual skills you acquired here and apply them, in deciding what kind of life you'll live and how you'll live that life. Courage, determination, the sense of your own capabilities, what you do with your education including the ideals you choose to serve—these are what *you* must now supply."

Close on an Inspiring, Congratulatory Note

Choose among the following:

- "Once again, thank you for inviting me. And to all of today's graduates, my warmest congratulations and best wishes. I hope that the degrees you've earned will be the stepping-stone to a lifetime of achievement, service, and success. This is *your* day, and it's great to be here to share with you."

- "President John F. Kennedy once said, 'Our goal is to again influence history instead of merely observing it.' I wish you great good fortune in doing exactly that: shape the forces of history and create a future that will make a difference— a difference in business, in your personal lives, and in this wonderful country to which we all owe so much."

- "Again, congratulations and best wishes to the Class of 20___. This is *your* day, and I thank you very much for inviting me to share it."

- "I hope that today's ceremonies—and the celebrations to follow—are a fitting end to one chapter in your lives … and the hopeful and promising beginning of another, full of new challenges, new successes, and new ways to learn and grow."

- "Again, thank you for inviting me to be with you, and once again, congratulations to all of you! For the Class of 20___, may this day be a joyous and fitting end to one chapter in your lives—and may it mark the hopeful beginning of another that will be filled with happiness and success."

- "And, now as you begin the next stage in your life, let me congratulate you once again ... and wish you the best of luck and all the success and happiness that life has to offer." *[End there or add:]* "Thank you, good luck, and Godspeed!"

For additional suggestions, see the next two sections.

19. College or University as an Alumnus or Alumna

Look over Section 18 again; some of the material applies. In addition, you can, during the introduction or as the topic of your entire speech, explain how the education you received there has benefited you. Another tack: comment on the institution's motto and on how relevant you have found it to be.

Here are some other suggestions.

Praise the Institution

■ "I'm proud to be an graduate of *[college/university]*. The caliber of students who attend is remarkable; the quality of the education that they receive here is also remarkable. Tomorrow's leaders in business, industry, government, and the professions are on campus today, and they're being trained in critical thinking and ethical values as well as in specific fields of knowledge."

Comment on Changes Since You Attended as Well as Enduring Qualities

■ "It's a very different *[name of institution]* from the one I graduated from years ago. *[Consider adding examples of changes.]* But the real essence of the institution remains the same: *[list its qualities]*. These are the qualities that have made *[institution]* so successful for so long. And they're going to be just as critical—if not more so—in the years ahead."

If the Institution Emphasizes Science, Note the Value of Humanistic Studies

■ "Scientist and philosopher Jacob Bronowski wrote that 'It is not the business of science to inherit the earth, but to inherit the moral imagination; because without that, man

and beliefs and science will perish together.'[2] My point is
that as you pursue scientific excellence you should never
ignore the value of literature, philosophy, music, history,
and the other humanistic studies. They light the way to the
'moral imagination' that Bronowski regarded as critical to
our fate."

If the Institution Does Very Well at Preparing Students for Life

■ "Grayson Kirk, the renowned educator, historian, and president of Columbia University, once said that 'Our greatest
obligation to our children is to prepare them to understand and to deal effectively with the world in which they
will live and not with the world *we* have known or the
world *we* would prefer to have.' *[Institution]* fulfills that
obligation exceptionally well/does a terrific job in that
area: it draws upon the eternal verities of *our past* ... to
prepare young people for *their* future. That is one of its
unique strengths—and the source of its enduring success."

If You're Receiving an Honorary Degree

■ "It's especially fitting—and satisfying—to receive one
more degree from my alma mater at this point in my life.
It's as if you're saying, '*[your first name]*, we think you've
done OK with the training we gave you.' It's truly gratifying
to know that, ___ years later, I still measure up to your high
standards."

2. Jacob Bronowski, *The Ascent of Man* (Boston: Little, Brown and Co.,
1973), p. 430.

20. Other Speeches at Academic Institutions

All the suggestions in Sections 18 and 19 are possibilities for speeches at other academic institutions. Here are some additional possibilities.

Comment on the Benefits of Contact Between Businesses and Academic Institutions

- "I always enjoy visiting a university and meeting with professors and students. It's stimulating; it really makes me feel younger. But beyond that, I want to give you a sense of what's happening 'out there,' an opportunity to complement your academic training and get an even better preparation for the transition the you face—the transition from learning to doing."

Comment on the Need for Collaboration Between Businesses and Academic Institutions

- "Campuses and corporations really do need to talk to each other; they need to build bridges—of cooperation, collegiality, and credibility."

Draw Parallels Between Business and Academia

- "There's an interesting and little-known similarity between businesses and institutions of higher learning: businesspeople, as well as academics, must live in a 'marketplace of ideas.' That's right: I live in an atmosphere/environment of intense competition among conflicting views of what the corporation's priorities should be, about how it should conduct itself, and about the nature of its obligations to its various stakeholders and to the society that allows it to exist and do business."

If Your Organization Has a Productive Relationship with the Academic Institution, You May Want to Comment on It

- "'Partners' is a word that we in the *[name of industry]* industry usually reserve for our dealers, suppliers, and our associates and joint ventures—people who share a direct interest in our business. But more and more these days, universities are our partners too." *[Explain how.]*

At Liberal-Arts Institutions, Consider Discussing the Impact of Liberal-Arts Values on Management

- "The points of view and skills taught in liberal-arts courses can make a major contribution to the evolution of an ethical and humanistic capitalism—a system that stimulates innovation, fosters excellence, benefits society, and dignifies work. Pressed as we managers may be by our day-to-day concerns, we must nevertheless serve this higher obligation as well—and we must find and develop the people who will help us to fulfill it."

Urge the Audience to Cultivate Breadth and Versatility

- "As you pursue your education, try to be both a specialist and a generalist, with a broad understanding of the relationship between disciplines. Why? Because in the real world of doing, the *application* of knowledge is far less compartmentalized than the *acquisition* of it."

Prepare the Audience for Differences Between Academic and Business Environments

- "There's a key difference between *learning* (generally an individual effort) and *doing*, which often requires you to develop a team whose members' talents complement and synergize each other, because no one individual can know everything that's needed to solve a problem."

Comment on the Importance of Lifelong Learning

- "Long after your formal training is over, you'll continue to learn, not only by osmosis from people in your own and other disciplines, but also from experience and observation. From some tasks that will turn out to be more (or less) difficult than you expected, from projects that will be great successes (or failures.) Always be asking yourself, 'Now what can I learn from that?'"

- "There are very few safe predictions about the years ahead. One of them is that the pace of technological change will continue to accelerate, which means you must prepare for a lifelong learning experience. It's the only way to avoid knowledge obsolescence. The most valuable skills you can acquire in college are curiosity—a personal 'culture of learning'—and the ability to absorb, analyze, and apply new information."

- "Companies like ours and institutions like yours really have no choice but to prepare people for a changing world in which the only constant is change itself."

- "In a time of rapid and sometimes unpredictable change, when tomorrow's answers are typically different from yesterday's (and even today's), your educational process has only just begun."

21. International Technical/ Technological Symposia

In most respects these speeches resemble addresses to a high-level group of professionals (see Section 22), with a few exceptions. International conferences are likely to be in historic, scenic places, so you might begin by commenting on your preconference experience with the locale.

This is a place to show respect and humility, especially if you're delivering the keynote. Refer to your colleagues as "this distinguished gathering."

A little research will help you find the first use of the technology in which the group is interested. You can use that as a springboard for a "how far we've come, how far we have to go" type of speech.

The audience is probably an elite group. If so, you can compliment them.

Example:

■ "Charles F. Kettering was the first and perhaps the greatest scientific mastermind at General Motors. He was a great inventor and thinker on research and innovation. He once remarked, 'The opportunities of man are limited only by his imagination. But so few have imagination that there are 10,000 fiddlers for each composer.'" *[You can then compare your audience to composers and talk about their creativity.]*

22. Conference of Fellow Professionals/Executives

In addition to the suggestions here, see Section 14.

Emphasize the Challenges That All Companies Face

■ "Some firms have made great progress; others, not so great. But I don't think the process ever ends. Every organization has to be in close and constant touch with its customers, so that its products reflect their tastes, preferences, and expectations. Every organization has to be working to involve every individual, directly and actively, in the success of the enterprise and to promote personal and vocational fulfillment of all its people. And every organization has to be relentlessly searching, within and outside, for new ways to cut lead times, exploit technology, and innovate faster."

End on an Encouraging Note About the Conference

■ "Thank you again for inviting me. It's been a pleasure to be with you, and I hope that this conference will be stimulating and productive for all of you."

If You're Closing out the Event

■ "I really/sincerely hope your conference—and by that I mean your personal experience—has been a good one. I hope it's been a stimulating and informative *[length of conference]* and that you'll come away with a better understanding of the issues, perhaps with some bright new ideas and powerful new approaches, and with about 20,000 volts of fresh enthusiasm for the challenges ahead."

23. Business School Lecture

B-school executive lectures are typically about the company and what it's doing right.

If Your Speech Is Part of a Lecture Series

- "It's a pleasure to be with you this morning/afternoon/evening and to take part in this distinguished lecture series."

If You've Been Invited More Than Once

- "It's a pleasure to be here in this outstanding school of business, and I'm delighted and honored to be asked to contribute once again to a truly distinguished lecture series. Being invited somewhere once is nice, but really, there's nothing quite so flattering as being asked back! It means you actually left them wanting more! I'll try to do the same thing today/tonight."

If Appropriate, Congratulate the School on Its High Standards or Rating

Example (if you're a graduate of that institution):

- "All of us connected with [school] can be very proud of what it's achieved, so let me congratulate all of you—students, faculty, and staff—on behalf of all of us alumni, whose belief that we made the right choice is once again confirmed! Clearly, one reason why [school] is so successful is that it's changing in the same ways as the business world for which it's preparing its students."

If You've Had a Chance to Talk with Students Beforehand

- "I love to be with business school students. I really like to hear what's on their minds as they absorb new knowledge and form their own approaches to business, management, and leadership. *[Perhaps quote what one or two of the students said to you.]* And maybe I can contribute to that process. Maybe I can complement your training with a few of my own thoughts and insights."

If You Talk About Your Company, Frame It as a Case Study

- "I've come here today with a case study to present. I'll confess that I didn't do a lot of reading, interviewing, and note-taking. In fact, I managed to do all of the research on the job."

To Lead into a Speech on Change

- "I see that your catalog *[or course list/executive seminar curriculum, etc.]* has a course entitled *[name of course on managing change]*. Well, that's a course that every manager in every organization in the world has signed up for, if not formally, at least in effect, because the key fact of life in business today really is *change*."

Emphasize the Skills That Your Organization Needs Business Schools to Provide.

- "In the high-tech, world-competitive 21st century, you just can't take years and years to cultivate the management abilities you need; things are changing much too fast. Today's managers have to come on board already equipped with well-developed people skills, a strong sense of corporate social responsibility, a good grasp of the interface between human beings and technology, a broad international perspective, and a clear understanding of innovation and strategic management." *[Add any other qualities you consider essential.]*

Emphasize the Importance of Understanding Customers and Markets

■ "A professional manager who jumps from one industry to another or pulls totally unrelated businesses together into a conglomerate may realize a measure of short-term financial gain. But who's the real innovator? Who's behind the creation of products and services that provide quality and value, that meet real needs? Who's responsible for the business growth that results in expanding job opportunities and a rising standard of living for millions of people? It's the person who immerses himself or herself in the *product* or *service*, in the *business*, in the customers and what they need now—and what they're going to need in the future. When someone asked Ray Kroc, the founder of McDonald's, about the secret to his success, Kroc said, 'It requires a certain kind of mind to see beauty in a hamburger bun.' He wasn't kidding. He was giving an example of one of the foundations of business success."

Emphasize the Importance of an Executive's Understanding Staff Functions

■ "To lead an organization, you really have to know it, inside out, including staff operations *[for manufacturing:* right down to the factory floor*]*. It's especially important to get a good grasp of advisory functions like legal, PR, and government relations, because political and social forces are, and will continue to be, a powerful influence on how the business is run."

Profess Your Love for Your Industry

The B-school speech is often a subtle recruiting pitch; thus:

■ "If you want a detached, objective view of the *[name of*

industry] industry, you've got the wrong person. I've been in this business for nearly ___ years and, if I had to do it all over, I would choose no other—because no other can match it for constant change, challenge, and all-around excitement. We're constantly finding great opportunities—brilliantly disguised as insoluble problems. And success, I've found, is simply a matter of penetrating the disguise."

At the conclusion, you can refer to this statement and compare the students' careers and yours:

■ "As you prepare for your own careers, the best I can wish for you is that 20 or 30 or even 40 years from now, you can look back at the road you've traveled and say to yourself, 'I would have chosen no other.'"

Also see material in Section 35 on innovation, another standard B-school speech topic.

24. Speeches to Charitable/Arts Foundations

Express Your Support for the Organization's Vision, Values, or Mission

- "It's a wonderful feeling for me to be here today/tonight, to be among all these luminaries and leaders and—especially—to share your commitment to *[purpose of the organization]*."

Praise the Organization for Its Effectiveness

Make the case using facts and numbers as appropriate. Finish with:

- "All of that happened because of the generosity of people like you, because of *your* conviction that you *could* and *would* make a difference and that, despite the many demands on your time and resources, you do indeed have the power to do something about the vast and complex problems of our society."

If there is a founder or guiding spirit, briefly praise his or her efforts. If the person is in the audience, you can speak directly to him or her at this point.

Congratulate the Organization on Any Recent Significant Accomplishments, Anniversaries, or Milestones

- "It's a great pleasure to be with you today/tonight as you celebrate your ___ anniversary/ ___ years of *[organization's mission] / [accomplishment] / [milestone]*."

Commend the Organization for Translating Ideals into Action

- "The poet James Russell Lowell once said that 'all the beautiful sentiments in the world weigh less than a single lovely action.'[3] He was so right. But *you* have converted your beautiful sentiments into countless lovely actions."

- "As we all know, every good idea ultimately degenerates into hard work. Well, *[name of project or organization]* is a good idea—no, make that a great idea—but without the hard work of everyone here, and many others as well, it would never have become the reality that it is today."

- "We all know that it's good to give of yourself, but it's getting from thought to action that stymies most of us. You've crossed that gap, and I applaud you for it."

- "Thank you for everything you've done to make people aware of the problem of _____—and thank you for everything you've done to solve it."

If Appropriate, Praise the Audience's Organizational Skills

- "They say that if you want to make sure that something gets done, ask a busy person. I couldn't agree more! It's busy people like you who have really mastered the art of organizing their time, focusing their energy, and getting more done than any 'un-busy' person would think possible."

Praise the Organization's Other Positive Qualities
Example:

- "I've always admired the idealism of *[name of organization]* people, especially their enduring belief that the future can be better than the past, because people get together and *make* it better. And I've always been impressed by their commitment ... and by their skill and professionalism."

3. "Rousseau and the Sentimentalists." If citing Lowell doesn't feel authentic, simply say, "Someone once said, ... " or "A very wise man once said, ... "

To lead into a discussion of these qualities:

■ "*[Institution]* is a vibrant [cultural/community] institution, with a future even brighter than its past. Maybe we've/you've been lucky—but I think that what we/you have here takes a lot more than luck."

If Appropriate, Praise the Organization's Adaptability

■ "A very wise man[4] once observed that you can never step into the same river twice—because that river is constantly flowing and changing. And you are always changing too: always responding—and hopefully anticipating—the needs of [whomever the organization serves]."

If the Organization Supports the Performing Arts

■ "An art critic[5] once observed that 'culture is a little like dropping an Alka-Seltzer into a glass—you don't see it, but somehow it does something.' That 'something,' whatever it is, is what we're seeking when we support and promote the performing arts. Long after a performance is over, we feel excited, elevated, inspired by what human beings are capable of. That feeling inspires us to develop our own potential and seek excellence in our own pursuits."

If the Organization Supports Children

■ "Joan Ganz Cooney, who founded the Children's Television Workshop, once remarked that 'Cherishing children is the mark of a civilized society.' We *are* a civilized society; cherishing children is what this organization is all about. [*Consider adding:* I'm *or* All of us at *[company]* are proud to be a part of it.]"

4. The Greek philosopher Heraclitus (6th century BCE).
5. Hans Magnus Enzensberger, quoted by Hans Haacke, *The New York Times*, January 25, 1987.

Point to the Impact of the Organization's Work

- "Just remember: 50 years from now it won't matter what kind of car you drove, what kind of house you lived in, how much you had in your bank account, or what your clothes looked like. But the world may be a little better because you *[did whatever the organization does]*."

If the Organization Supports the Less Fortunate, Express a Personal Perspective
Example:

- "The more I've seen of the world, the more I've realized how many people really do have the will and desire to make it, but somehow life and circumstances have failed to meet them halfway. I see these people and I think, 'There but for the grace of God …'—because I wonder how many of them could be where *I* am if only they'd had the opportunities I've had … and I wonder just where *I'd* be if I'd gone through life in their shoes. It's not fair, but that's how it is."

If You've Been Asked to Solicit Contributions

- "So please give generously *[to name of campaign]*, because you really can help. And you *will* help—perhaps more than you can ever know."
- "The problems, the challenges, the need—they never go away. And if they don't, neither can we."

Close on a Hopeful Note, Possibly Connected to the Organization's Mission or Values

- "My best wishes for another year of progress toward *[organization's mission/goal]*."

   For additional ideas, see the next section.

25. Trade, Professional, or Industry Association

The content will probably be largely driven by your organization's strategic and PR agendas and/or by your assigned topic. Nevertheless, the way you handle the amenities and talk about the challenges facing the profession or industry as a whole can make a big difference in the way your message is heard.

Open by Praising the Organization

■ "Thank you [*if appropriate:* for inviting me to be one of your keynoters … and] for giving me the opportunity to address this distinguished organization."

You may also want to note how long the organization has been around:

■ "I'm pleased and honored to have been invited to address this distinguished organization that's now in its [*number*] year of service to the [*name of industry or profession*]."

Open by Mentioning Your Personal Ties to the Organization

■ "I'm delighted to be here with so many colleagues and friends."

Mention the Organization You Represent

■ "I'm delighted to represent _____ before this important industry group [*perhaps comment on why the group is important*] and to talk about [*topic*]."

Make a Positive Statement About the Communications Opportunity

■ "I want to thank [*name*] for inviting me to be your

keynoter/speaker today. It's rare that we get so many top
people from all across the industry together in one place
and, *[name of person who invited you]*, you've given me a terrific communication opportunity that I really do appreciate."

■ "It's a pleasure to be with you today *[if appropriate:* to
deliver the keynote address at this important conference]. I
am really looking forward to saying some things that I feel
very strongly about—and saying them to some of the very
people who are in the best position to act on my message."

Open with a Reference to Your Assigned Topic
Example:

■ "Good morning/afternoon/evening and welcome! In the
next *[length of conference]* days, we're going to be doing a
lot of thinking and talking about 'New Ways to Achieve
Success in the Marketplace.' So I'd like to open up with a
really basic question: *why* are we looking for 'new ways' to
succeed? Why did the *[name of organizing committee]*, in its
infinite wisdom, select this topic as an umbrella for our
presentations and panel discussions? The simple answer is
that the old ways of doing business don't work any more.
And one reason *why* the old ways don't work is that ...
[explain why]."

If the Organization Has Come a Long Way in a Short
Time

■ "*[If appropriate:* I'm delighted—and *honored*—to deliver
your keynote speech tonight.] This event and the audience
in front of me are a vivid reminder of the progress we've
over the last few years. Only ___ years ago, the idea of a
conference like this would have been nothing more than a
dream in someone's fertile imagination."

Emphasize What the Audience Members Have in Common

The members of the audience obviously know what they all have in common, but they like to hear it repeated and reaffirmed:

- "One thing that impresses me about this association is its striking diversity. You come from various professions/organizations *[list examples]*. And yet you're all here because you face the same challenges—and because you believe that there are broad principles, as well as specific solutions, that one group can share with another."
- "I know what a wide range of companies and interests we have in this industry. We have strong opinions and there are many things we don't agree on. Sometimes it seems there's almost *nothing* we agree on! But there's one thing we all *can* agree on: that a growing *[name of industry]* industry is good for all of us. So anything we do, as individual companies or as a group, that drives industry sales is good for *all* of us."

Or, more briefly:

- "If there's one thing that binds us all together, it's the fact that we ...."

Note that even though your business is different from those of many of your listeners, you nevertheless face the same problems:

- "The issues I'll discuss are critical to the health and future of our business—and, as I'll show, they have serious implications for yours as well."

Consider Making a Relevant Reference to the Wording of the Invitation
Example:

- "I'm grateful for this invitation—and I'm relieved, too, that you invited me here to talk about 'challenges and opportunities'—and not 'solutions.' I really don't have any simple solution to our problems—and neither, I dare say, does anybody else."

Urge Active Participation in the Conference

- "*[Name of organization]* meetings have traditionally been characterized by candor, open debate and discussion, and a freewheeling exchange of ideas. We have, in effect, many lifetimes of knowledge and experience in this room. There's so much we can learn from each other. So, enter in and don't be shy."

To Emphasize the Importance of Time and to Create a Sense of Urgency

Whatever you think the industry, profession, organization, or movement needs to do, you can encourage prompt action:

- "Peter Drucker put it in a very stark terms: 'The supply of time is totally inelastic. … Time is totally perishable and cannot be stored. … Time is totally irreplaceable …. There is no substitute for time.'[6] As our industry grows more complex and more competitive with each passing year, these really are lessons that we must learn over and over again."
- "We've made some important beginnings, but we have to do more. The world is changing too fast. *We've* got to

6. *The Effective Executive*, Chapter 2.

change—and faster—because we're facing some very tough challenges." [Optional: Explain those challenges.]

To Lead into Your Agenda of Action Items for the Profession or Industry

- "There's a great quote from Francis Bacon; you may have heard it: 'He that will not apply new remedies must accept new evils: for time is the greatest innovator.'[7] Bacon had it exactly right: the important thing is to move forward. There *will* be change, whether we like it or not. So what can we do to make sure that the changes turn out to our liking?"

Call for Industry-Wide Entrepreneurship

- "We're going to need even more worker participation, more management creativity, more innovative contributions from our subsidiaries and high-tech partners—more entrepreneurship of every kind—to meet our objectives in the years ahead."

Urge the Industry to Speak with a Single Voice

- "The key to winning in the marketplace of ideas is to find the points we agree on and make sure that on those issues we speak with a single, loud, insistent, and *consistent* voice … because really, we're all in this together."

Emphasize the Importance of Professional Training

- "We must plan and prepare today, to ensure that when you/[*organization*] hold(s) your/its 50th or 60th annual [*name of occasion*], the room will be filled with people as bright and as skilled, as capable and as creative, as those who are here tonight."

7. "Of Innovations," *Essays or Counsels, Civil and Moral.*

If Your Speech Has Been Largely About Your Company's Challenges

- "Our experience has some lessons for any company going through tough times. *[Example of discussion that might follow this statement:]* One of them is that you need quality products/services and people. Those are the foundation, and any company that doesn't have them had better get busy and develop them. Then you need clear, focused strategies that grow directly out of who you are and what you do well. And you need the courage to make a few bold moves—which, almost by definition, will not be popular. With all of that, when the bad times are over, you can end up being even stronger than you ever were before."

Conclude by Calling for a Commitment to Industry Growth

- "Here is what I want each of you to do before you leave this room: I want each of you to make a silent, personal, *unshakable* commitment to growth. Tell yourself that you *believe* in growth, that you *can* grow, and that from this moment forth, you will *commit* yourself to growth … and you will *commit* yourself to drawing upon all the talent and creativity in your organizations and in our industry … and to taking the creative risks that will help you to grow. And then let us work and *grow together*."

Conclude by Calling for Cooperation Among the Professions and Disciplines in the Organization

- "There's a reason why astronomical observatories are located in every region of the globe: astronomers know that there's no place on earth from which the entire sky can be seen. Not one of us sees the whole picture; none of us has all the answers. We can all get tremendous benefits out of combining our resources and working together toward the goals we all share."

- "A true partnership isn't easy. It requires give and take on both sides, and when some see just how much giving will be necessary, they may get cold feet. But, believe me, there never was a worse time for cold feet. We have to realistically assess our challenges—together. And we have to go forward—together—because there's so much we can achieve—together."

- "This association has the opportunity to build bridges among groups that still need to understand each other a lot better. And I urge you to build those bridges. Get involved in open, honest discussion with your counterparts and colleagues. Imagine yourself in the other person's shoes. Get to know each other better. Build confidence and trust. Replace confrontation with cooperation."

- "We've made some very encouraging beginnings, and this conference is going to help us [*or, if your speech is at the end:* has helped us] discover where we need to go from here. So let's work together and get the job done."

- "In order to build demand for our products/services, we have to build *partnerships*—partnerships grounded in the needs of the customer/client/end user … and inspired by our vision of what we can achieve together!"

- "The more we/you work together, the stronger we'll/you'll be."

- "Let me close this talk by *opening* a new dialogue among our companies, among us as people. Let's commit ourselves to creating new initiatives, new ideas, and new ways to join together and work together to [*achieve whatever goal you're advocating*]." [*Optional: Make some commitment or pledge, something to start the dialogue.*]

26. Financial Presentations to Board of Directors or Outside Analysts

If your organization is large enough for you to be giving this kind of speech, then the information and perhaps a draft (or at least an outline) of the speech will come from your internal Finance or Investor Relations people (or an outside Investor Relations consultant). The initial speech draft (or other input) may be written in financial jargon, in which case you should rewrite it according to your own natural speaking style. (See Sections 46 and 49.) This speech can be both dignified and conversational. It doesn't have to sound like a computer talking.

As regards intent and content, the presentation should provide proof and reassurance that you understand your industry, competition, and markets and that your (or management's) strategy will increase shareholder value and enable your organization to meet or exceed its obligations to the community and to society.

Also, consider putting your personal stamp on the board/analyst speech by doing one or more of the following.

Begin with a Clear Overview
- "I'll begin today's presentation with a review of our historical performance, our financial targets, and the major environmental trends that affect us."
- [More formal:] "I'm pleased to have this opportunity to present to you an account of our stewardship of [company] in 20__."

Inject the Human Element

■ "Today/this morning/this afternoon, I'd like to tell you how we've been able to *[whatever the organization's accomplishments are]*. Beyond that, I hope to convey to you some of the excitement and enthusiasm of our people, as they come to understand the implications of what we've been doing."

Other ways to inject the human element: praise specific groups and individuals for good results or recount brief interactions with individuals in the audience or in the organization. (These mini-anecdotes don't have to be funny—just personal and relevant to the point you're trying to make.)

If Progress Has Been Slow, Ask for Patience

■ "As we continue to go after the opportunities that still lie ahead, we ask for your help, your patience, and, most of all, your support."

27. Suppliers, Retailers, Clients, Brokers, or Other Business Partners

A speech to your business partners may take place at a meeting with the management of another company or with the senior executives of a group of such companies. The speech may be part of a larger agenda, such as an industry conference, in which case it's important to find out in advance what the other speakers are going to say, so that you're aware of any potential inconsistencies with or repetitions of what you're going to say.

Whatever the circumstances or agenda, you'll want to consider spending at least some time talking about trust, interdependence, and partnership.

Show Enthusiasm with a Strong Opening

- "Thank you, *[name of introducer]*. Good afternoon, everyone, and welcome. It's great to see you, and I'm glad you could all take time out of your busy schedules to be here today."
- "It's great to see so many of our friends in the industry—and top people from our company—all together in one place."
- *[If entertainment is to follow:]* "On behalf of all of us at *[organization]*, I'm delighted to welcome you to what promises to be an outstanding evening of fellowship and entertainment."
- "*[If true:* I get a number of requests to give speeches, but I especially appreciate this one.*]* It's not often I get to speak to some of our most important customers and some of our key suppliers—at the same time."
- "In my __ years in the *[name of industry/profession]* indus-

try/profession, I have never seen such an exciting time!"

- "As you can tell, I'm just delighted to be here with all of you."

- "It's a real pleasure to see so many faces that are now familiar to me from all our day-to-day business dealings ... and the many events and functions that we've attended together. I always say, it's all about relationships. And as we work together year after year, it's great to see how close we've become, as business partners—and as friends."

Establish a Bond with the Audience by Explaining the Benefits for All

- "We're partners in progress, we're partners in profit, and we're partners in a vital and exciting business."

- "This meeting/conference is a wonderful opportunity to spend time together and talk about the issues that face us all."

- *[To clients/customers/end users:]* "Knowing what's on your minds helps us to serve you better."

- *[To industry colleagues:]* "We hope you've come to look forward to these conferences as much as we have. They give us a chance to spend time together, take stock of where we've been and where we're headed, and talk about the issues that face us all."

Show Appreciation for Customers/Clients/End Users

- "We very much appreciate your business—and we're committed to continuing to earn it, in 20__ and beyond."

This theme can be the beginning of a speech that lays out the company's customer/client/end user strategy:

- "We're going to earn your business by ...."

For a Conference That Involves Sports, Consider a Relevant Sports Metaphor

■ "I know I'm in a room full of tennis and golf enthusiasts, so you're all aware of the importance of making proper contact with the ball. Proper contact is a key issue in our business, too. An awful lot depends on happens at that crucial moment of contact between our organization and yours."

Create a Link Between Change and Opportunity

■ "Today we have new ways to find out what consumers want and need; new technologies for developing, producing, and distributing our products; and new media that enable us to interact and build relationships with our consumers. What all of this means is fantastic new opportunities for manufacturers to create value for retailers, for every trading partner to create value throughout the supply chain, and for all of us—as companies and as individuals— to build true strategic partnerships."

■ "It's a whole new world, a very different environment from what some of us experienced 20 or 25 years ago. It's a world in which the ground rules have been radically rewritten. It's a world of much higher expectations … and many more opportunities."

Ask for Suggestions and Ideas; Make a Connection Between Input and Success

■ "As we go forward, we want your comments and input, so that we know for sure that we're on track and doing everything we can to help *you* to be more profitable."

■ "We're like two people in a three-legged race: the only way we can win is to work together in perfect synch!"

■ "We need you to help us [*if appropriate*: continue to] cut costs, grow the business, and create sustainable competitive advantage."

- "I'd be the first to admit that we don't have all the answers. So please tell us what's on your minds. What have we done wrong? What have we done right? How can we make our partnership stronger?"

- "Please, tell us how we can work together more effectively. Knowledge really is power, and the more we share it, the more successful we'll be."

Ask Your Business Partners to Help You Innovate

- "There are lots of bold moves we can make, breakthrough strategies that will leave our competitors sitting in the dust and thinking, 'Darn! Now why didn't we think of that?' Help us find them. Help us deliver the quality and innovation that our business success depends on."

- "We need business partners who are committed to us, who will come to us with new ideas and opportunities."

Praise Them for Having Helped You Innovate

- "Each of you has helped us build our business with innovative ideas that have delivered enormous cost savings and given us a real competitive edge."

Emphasize the Value of Trust Across the Supply Chain

- "If you really want to work together with your trading partners to develop new and more efficient ways to bring products to market, you must be able to ask yourself, 'What would we do if we were one company? What if we were all focused on what we could do *together* to reduce the cost of bringing goods to market?' And to be able to engage in that kind of open dialogue with your trading partners, you really have to have trust."

■ "True partnerships based on trust can open up all kinds of opportunities for reconsidering our make/buy decisions—and in fact for challenging all kinds of assumptions about how our business works best."

Urge the Audience to Think Differently About Alliances and Partnerships

■ "The strongest barrier to true strategic alliances is in our own minds, in the form of 'the tyranny of the status quo.'"

■ "*Of course* disagreements will arise. But if we're really going to make progress, trade-offs must be made, and both parties must ultimately agree on a course of action that benefits them both."

You can go further with this theme: ask the audience for a commitment to partnership.

■ "So let us begin, right now, today, to break down that mental barrier. Let us be willing to test the limits. Let us realize that our current safe boundaries were once unknown frontiers. Here is what I want each of you to do before you leave this room. I want each of you to make a silent, personal, unshakable commitment to building stronger, more open business relationships. Tell yourself that each week, or each month, you will do one thing, whether big or small, to build trust with your trading partners."

If You've Asked the Audience to Do Things

If you've asked the audience to take action, you might cap off your speech with the following:

■ "Finally, we need you to do all of the above with a spirit of teamwork, partnership, and trust—and a sense of urgency."

In a Speech to Customers/Clients/Retailers/Dealers, Close with a Commitment

- "We do so much appreciate your business … and we're determined to keep earning it—and to earn *more* of it."

Close by Praising the Audience

- "With winners like you on our team, it's clear that the best is yet to come!"

Close with a Call for Unity

- "Let us work, create value, and grow … together."
- "All of us at *[company/organization]* look forward to working more closely with you, as our industry enters a new era of great promise and exciting opportunity."

Close with Good Wishes

- "I wish you every success in taking advantage of the many exciting opportunities that lie ahead."

Close with Optimism

- "We've only just begun. We've just begun to explore the possibilities for pursuing excellence, building our partnership, and breaking new ground in cost, quality, and innovation."

If You're Speaking Near the Beginning of a Year

If you're speaking near the beginning of a year, you can close with the following:

- "I know it's going to be a great year for all of us, a year of working together, to serve customers/clients/end users and grow our businesses … a year of innovation, profitability, and success."

Part Four

Specific Speech Situations

Each section of Part Four is devoted to a particular type of speech whose content is driven less by what the audience has in common and more by the audience's expectations, the situation, or the speech topic (or perhaps all three).

28. Keynote Speeches (Internal or External)

These speeches set the tone for an event or conference. They're expected to be thoughtful and inspirational. Since attention spans and enthusiasm are high, the keynote is an excellent opportunity to showcase your speaking skills, get your message across, and excite everyone about the rest of the event.

Speak very little about your company or organization, unless the subject is truly relevant to the keynote. Less is more.

The material in Sections 15 and 25 will give you ideas for themes you can develop.

Express Appreciation

- "I'm honored to be the keynote speaker for this distinguished program."
- "I'm delighted that you've asked me to deliver the keynote address. It's an excellent opportunity to talk about some of the issues that concern all of us."

Tell How the Keynote Word or Phrase—the Conference Theme—Excited You
Examples:

- "I looked at the conference title, your keynote—*[whatever the keynote is]*—immediately began ringing loud and clear in my ears, and I knew exactly what I wanted to say to you today."
- "Your conference theme—'The Spirit of Cooperation'—is the keynote I'll be sounding in my remarks today. I consider that spirit absolutely essential to the welfare of our nation/industry."

Create Excitement and Anticipation for Speakers Who Will Follow You

- "Today we have some are highly knowledgeable, thoughtful, and stimulating presenters who will elaborate on and reinforce these themes I've laid out ... and they'll provide additional approaches and actions you can take to *[accomplish whatever the goals of the conference are]*."

In Your Conclusion, Look Forward to the End of the Event

What do you hope the audience will gain from the event?

- "I urge you to make most of this conference and to leave here with a head full of new ideas, a handful of new tools, and a heart full of revitalized enthusiasm and determination for new and greater achievements. And I wish you every success."

- "It's going to be an exciting [day, week, etc.] of new ideas and experiences, and I hope you'll come away with *[hoped-for result]*."

If You're Closing the Conference, Give the Audience a Positive Sendoff

- "Thank you for inviting me. I wish you a successful and enjoyable conference."

- "I thank you again for your invitation. I hope that your conference is productive and stimulating, and that its rewards are felt long after it has ended."

- "I wish you every success in taking advantage of the many exciting opportunities that I know lie ahead."

- "Good luck! Thank you for inviting me, and I hope this conference has been your best ever!"

- "Thank you ... and have a great [day, week, etc.]!"

29. Panel Remarks

Your speech is one of several short presentations. The usual length is five to 10 minutes. The other panelists may be from different fields (e.g., academia, government) or they may be from competitor companies. Preparation and research are key: if you have some idea as to what others plan to say, you can avoid repetition and handle potential conflicts with your own speech.

If possible, speak first or last. If you speak first, you'll get to lay out the basic issues and others will seem to be echoing you. If you speak last, you're more likely to be remembered.

You'll typically be asked to represent your organization or your industry and give its position on the panel topic. Always be sure you understand the topic and make your speech relevant to it.

In your remarks, take a broad view: try to show who else benefits or stands to benefit from what your organization is doing or planning to do. It's OK to plug your organization—but *briefly*, *subtly*, and *in connection with the panel topic*.

Here are two additional suggestions.

Praise the Moderator and/or Your Fellow Panelists as Equals

■ "I'm very much aware that I've been preceded on this podium by a number of highly eminent speakers. I'm delighted to be in their company—and to address this distinguished group."

Consider Ending by Stating What You Hope the Panel Discussion Will Achieve

■ *[State overall, higher goal, then say:]* "I hope today's discussion will help us to do just that."

30. IPO Announcements

While the actual legal and financial content of your presentation will be largely determined by others and the numbers and other nuts-and-bolts information will be included in the printed documents, you can nevertheless (if circumstances seem appropriate) make the speech an expression of your personal feelings about the accomplishment—and thank the people who deserve credit for bringing it about.

Make every effort to accentuate the personal element and avoid impersonal language and bureaucratic jargon. (See Sections 46 and 49.)

Discuss the size and significance of the IPO. Express a sense of accomplishment that the job is done. Consider mentioning everybody who played a major role—senior managers, lawyers, outside financial advisors, and investment bankers. Make each group feel good about its contribution. If appropriate, congratulate the team of leaders on how well they have worked together to bring the IPO about.

Begin with a Formal Announcement (if No One Else Has Done So)

■ "This is a great day for [company]—our first day as a publicly traded company. Today, at [exact time], our symbol, ___, crossed the ticker of [name of stock exchange] for the very first time."

Briefly Review the Company History, Positioning the IPO as the Next Logical Development

■ "When we founded [company] in [year], our ambition was to see it flourish and grow ... and one day float/be traded on [name of stock exchange]."

Thank the People Responsible for Your Success Thus Far

■ "My deepest thanks to all of the great *[name of company]* people who have built such a successful business/institution/organization and brought us to where we are today."

Talk About the Positive Reaction from the Financial/Investment Community

■ "*[Company]* is a great business with an excellent growth record and I am delighted that sophisticated and knowledgeable investors want to share in its long-term future."

Talk Optimistically About the Future

■ "I am absolutely delighted/*so* pleased to be part of *[company]* as it embarks on the next stage of its life—as a publicly traded company—and I look forward to welcoming all our new shareholders on board. *[If appropriate:* We have a great management team in place and a unique and innovative culture.*]* We'll keep working to grow the business, to create value for our shareholders, and to provide outstanding products/services to our customers/clients/end users."

31. Emceeing a Conference ("Continuity")

Find out from the conference organizers exactly what is expected of you. Your role is to keep everything moving smoothly. There will be various activities and breaks, which you will announce, either *ad lib* or with some of the following phrases.

Welcome Everyone and Create a Sense of Excitement and Anticipation

■ "Good morning/afternoon/evening, everyone! It's great to see you … and what an incredible day/afternoon/evening we have planned!"

Praise the Locale
Example:

■ "I can't think of a better way to get away from the cold and snow than to be here in sunny Hawaii."

Bring on a Speaker or Entertainer

■ "Our first/next/last speaker is _____. *[Optional: introduce the speaker's content.]* He'll/she'll explain … *[short reference to theme of speech].*"

If You'll Be Returning, Announce That Fact

■ "At the end of the program, I'll be back to offer some concluding thoughts. *[If appropriate:* Now let me introduce our first guest speaker.*]*"

■ "After our guest speaker, I'll be back with some closing comments."

Thank a Speaker or Entertainer

■ "Thanks, Jim. That was very informative/stimulating/etc."

You can follow this with a short summary of what the person achieved:

■ "And I think that in just a few minutes, you've given everybody a much better understanding of … [*or*: you've inspired us to …, *etc.*]."

Bring on the Next Presenter

■ "And now, we're going to hear from … [*next speaker*]. [*Optional: introduce the speaker's content.*] He/she will explain … [*short reference to theme of speech*]."

Announce a Break

■ "And now we'll take a 30-minute/etc. break, after which … [*whatever is to follow the break*]."

Break for a Meal

■ "Thank you—and enjoy your dinner/etc.!"

Consider mentioning something coming later, to create a sense of anticipation:

■ "A little later in our program, [*tell them what will happen*]. But for now, enjoy your lunch/dinner/etc.—and thank you all for being here with us today."

■ "Well, now it's time to break for lunch/dinner/etc. I hope you'll enjoy your meal … [and have a relaxing afternoon,] because tonight … [*etc.*]."

Thank the Person/People Who Made the Conference Possible
Examples:

■ "And now it's my pleasure to introduce someone who is already familiar to most—if not all—of you. Without his/her efforts, we would not be here tonight. Let's all show our appreciation for … [*name*]."

- "I'd like to shine the spotlight for a moment on someone who has been working hard behind the scenes to make all of this work out so well. So, now let's thank … *[name]*."

Close Out the Event, with Comments if Appropriate

- "All good things must come to an end, and it's time to wind up our conference. *[If appropriate:* So I'd just like to leave you with a few closing thoughts.*]*"
- "Clearly, our conference had all the key elements of success:
  - *information* about what's going on in our organization;
  - *action* that we can take, as individuals and as members of *[name of group]*;
  - and *inspiration* to act on the information … and do what needs to be done."
- "Well, it's been quite a day/week, and I hope you've gotten as much out of it as we've tried to put into it. We've tried to give you plenty of information and inspiration—food for the left brain and food for the right. And we've tried to make it all both stimulating and fun—not an easy combination to achieve—and we owe our thanks to everybody who planned this year's event." *[Optional: single out individuals.]*

32. The Annual Meeting/Shareholder Speech

This is another speech that's typically composed by others in the organization (often Finance people and lawyers). Its content is pretty strictly dictated by the company's performance and strategies.

Nevertheless, you have some opportunities to keep it from being an impersonal, totally robotic recitation. Wherever possible, speak to the shareholders about the organization in personal terms—"your company," "our company," and "we"—instead of "XYZ Corporation" or "the company." Also consider the following amenities and ways of personalizing the speech.

Welcome Everyone

■ "Good morning/afternoon, ladies and gentlemen. I am *[name and title]*. On behalf of the Board and all of our management team, I would like to extend a warm welcome to each of you, and I thank you for attending our ___ *[e.g., 48th]* Annual Meeting of Stockholders. Let me now report on the state of your corporation."

If appropriate, recognize and greet key individuals.

If Appropriate, Thank the Shareholders for Their Support

Note that this approach is only "if appropriate." If the stock is plummeting, for example, it is a crisis situation and you have an entirely different speechwriting task. Obviously, this is not a book about crisis communications. We are assuming more normal circumstances for these executive presentations.

■ "I want to thank all of you who have supported *[company]* over the years, contributed to its competitiveness and strength, and given it your vote of confidence with your investments. Our management team is doing—and will do—everything is in its power to see that those investments increase in value."

Open with an Overview of Your Talk
Example:

■ "And now, as is our custom, I'd like to present a brief overview of the state of your corporation. My remarks today are a story of continuity and change: continuity of the programs and strategies that we laid out for ourselves [e.g., *at the beginning of this decade*] … and change that has brought us closer to our goals."

Share Credit for the Company's Performance (if Good)

■ "One of the great advantages of this job is that I've met some of the finest people you'll find anywhere: our customers/clients and our service providers, who are some of the sharpest businesspeople and most capable and innovative entrepreneurs in the world … and, of course, there are the people everywhere in our organization. I've always been impressed by their outstanding adaptability, creativity, and hard work. They've shown plenty of grace under pressure. My hat's off to them—I just can't praise them enough."

Consider Closing on a Personal Note

For example, talk about how gratifying your tenure as CEO has been for you.

■ "If I were to sum it all up in a very few words, I'd say that I've spent ___ years in the best job in the world. It's been a great honor for me to help guide this great organization through some of the most exciting years our industry has ever known. It's been frustrating at times, challenging *all* the time, and enormously gratifying, because when you really work at something, you can see the changes taking place. It's just like Teddy Roosevelt said: 'Far and away the best prize that life offers is the chance to work hard at work worth doing.'"

If Possible, Close on an Optimistic Note

■ "We're well positioned for growth, and I'm exceedingly optimistic about the future."

Consider Closing with a Strong Statement of Your Company's Mission

■ "All of us at *[company]* are working hard to earn your support and confidence. We're conscious of our many responsibilities—social, fiduciary, and economic. And as we work to fulfill them, we will never lose sight of our primary mission— *[reiterate your mission and consider adding, "… and thus to provide job security for our people, total satisfaction for our customers/end users, and a superior return on investment for you, our stockholders"]*."

Reminder: Wherever Possible, Avoid Jargon and Speak Naturally

■ *Not this:* "Additionally, we have implemented extensive product improvements."
■ *But this:* "We've made a lot of changes in our products, too."

Also see Sections 46 and 49.

33. Speaking to Managers or Other Executives (Internal or External) About Quality or Productivity

There are many different schools of thought on quality and productivity, as well as company-specific approaches to these subjects, so you'll most likely be speaking in terms of your organization's approach and its basic definitions of quality/productivity concepts.

Such speeches are also partly motivational. They may incorporate any of several themes. For example, it may be relevant to candidly describe your quality/productivity position versus the competition and the industry. Also, you might want to explain how quality is central to your brand, product, or service image. Another useful argument, if applicable to your situation, is the compatibility of quality and productivity: solving quality problems often leads to greater efficiency.

In internal speeches, praise outstanding quality/productivity gains by audience members, groups of audience members, or individuals. Urge the audience members to think about satisfying—even anticipating—the needs of the internal customers for their product or service.

Other possibilities:

Note the Quality Expectations of Your Customers or End Users

■ "Consumers/clients/consumers today do not tolerate slipups of any kind—on quality, on availability, on anything. Perfect execution is now the price of entry. They expect more from us—and more from our products/services."

Mention the Connection Between Productivity Savings and Growth

■ "Productivity is *everyone's* job. Why is productivity so important? Because we can invest the productivity savings in growth initiatives—and achieve the all-important *profitable* growth that's so key to our success."

Explain How the Organization Can Be Proactive on Quality

■ "Two tasks must be accomplished. First, everyone in the organization has to get on the same wavelength; we must have a clear, simple language of quality, so that we are all using the same words for the same things. And second, we need to get from the abstract to the concrete—to move from the quality ideal to the specific procedures, processes, and behaviors that produce quality."

Talk About the "Holistic" Nature of Quality

Quality comes from everywhere in the system. Emphasize the contribution of each individual at every level. Discuss personal, individual responsibility for quality:

■ "Success doesn't depend on implementing this program or that. Instead, it begins and ends with people—people who take personal individual responsibility for quality, people who are willing to make tough decisions that maximize quality regardless of schedule pressures, people who, when they see something wrong, have the courage and team spirit to do something about it, even if it's not covered in the procedures manual, and above all, people who are ready to stop saying 'they' and start saying 'I' … as in 'How can *I* be part of the solution?'"

■ "There's only one way to respond to all the change going

on around us—and that is to change ourselves, to be tire-less in the search for new paths to quality and productivity."

- "It's been many, many years since W. Edwards Deming made his great revelation—that the major share of the responsibility for quality was to be attributed not to work-ers, but to management. Today that revelation has been translated into mainstream practice: we all realize that world-class quality can be produced only by people who have been encouraged to be quality leaders. If we focus only on product and process, our gains will be limited by the physical constraints of our equipment. But where peo-ple have been trained to be quality leaders, where progress depends on attitude and behavior change, the possibilities are essentially open-ended!"

34. Introducing a New Product or Technology

The content of this speech will be dictated mainly by the occasion and innovation itself. Here are a few suggestions.

Set the stage by showing a clear market need and competitive edge. Make connections between customer wants/needs and product/service benefits. Thank individuals and groups responsible for the achievement. You may want to discuss the broader implications of the innovation: explain how it will benefit many of the company's stakeholders and, of course, how it advances the company's strategy.

Examples:

- "It's one more example of our constant effort to make things better, to solve problems, to create the future."
- "The product we're introducing today is part of a threefold mission: to care for our customers, to care for the environment, and to be the industry's technology leader."

As always, keep the language clear, simple, and personal. I mention this because the original information about the innovation may come from technical people and you may need to modify it, in terms of both style and vocabulary, in order to make an effective oral presentation. (See Sections 46 and 49.)

35. Speaking About Innovation

Your personal and organizational views and the way your profession or industry sees the importance of innovation will largely decide your subject matter.

In internal speeches, you might want to explain the relationship between innovation and the organization's success. Give examples of new products and/or services that have grown the business or even taken the industry in a different direction.

The phrases in this section illustrate other points you might want to make.

Distinguish Between "Invention" and "Innovation"

■ "Back in the late 19th and early 20th centuries, there was a great German chemist named Johann von Baeyer. He made many contributions to science and, in 1905, he was awarded a Nobel Prize. One morning, Baeyer came into his laboratory and found that his assistants had built an ingenious mechanical stirring device operated by water turbines. The professor was fascinated by the complex machine and he summoned his wife from their apartment next door. For a while, she watched the apparatus in silent admiration. And then she exclaimed, 'What a lovely idea for making mayonnaise!'[1] There's a basic distinction here: his assistants were the *inventors*—but his wife was the *innovator*. As Peter Drucker says,[2] 'Above all, innovation is not invention. It is a term of economics rather than of technology. The measure

1. Clifton Fadiman (ed.), *The Little, Brown Book of Anecdotes* (Little Brown & Co., 1985), p. 13.
2. In *People and Performance: The Best of Peter Drucker on Management* (HarperCollins, 1977).

of innovation is the impact on the environment.'
Innovation, according to Drucker, 'allows resources the
capacity to create wealth.'"

Short version:

■ "Peter Drucker says that the difference between 'innovation' and 'invention' is that 'innovation' is 'a term of economics rather than of technology' and that 'the measure of
innovation is the impact on the environment .... [To manage innovation a manager has to be at least literate with
respect to the dynamics of innovation.']"

Explain How Technology Creates Wealth

■ "Technological innovation is, to quote the title of a book,[3]
the 'lever of riches.' Why is innovation so critical? Because
it's the raw material for the creation of prosperity and a
better quality of life; everything else is just reshuffling and
redistribution of what we already have. Just as a lever dra-
matically increases the amount of force you can exert, so
innovation increases productivity, spurs economic growth,
and raises everyone's quality of life."

Additional material on this point:

■ "The ancient Greeks gave us the lever, the wedge, the pul-
ley, and the gear. The Romans gave us horseshoes and the
Chinese gave us stirrups; these two inventions revolution-
ized transportation and warfare. In the Middle Ages, people
developed the chimney, which facilitated home cooking
and allowed us to get presents from Santa Claus. Islamic
society brought paper to Europe from China. And from the

3. Joel Mokyr, *The Lever of Riches: Technological Creativity and
Economic Progress* (Oxford University Press, 1990).

Chinese, we also got the umbrella and the toothbrush. My point is that many of what now seem to us to be the most mundane of contraptions actually had a profound effect on human progress. The prosperity, comforts, and living standards we enjoy today are built upon thousands of years of innovations, many of which are now so common that it's hard to think that there was a time when they didn't exist."

Discuss the Broader Social Implications of Innovation

This topic is appropriate for external speeches.

- "The more we nurture innovation, the more we become what Peter Drucker calls 'an entrepreneurial society in which innovation and entrepreneurship are normal, steady, and continual …, an integral, life-sustaining activity in our organizations, our economy, our society.'[4] Such a society never needs to fear the future: it is creating it, every day."

Emphasize That True Innovation Can Occur Anywhere

Make the point that innovation can occur in any function, at any level, if people are given the freedom to be creative about the way they do their jobs and advance the organization toward its goals.

- "All of us need to establish an innovation mindset throughout the length and breadth of the organization—a mindset that sees innovation as something that everyone is capable of, as a progressive renewal that goes on in every activity of the business. It's something that everyone wants to get involved in, because, ideally, each individual knows that the more competitive the organization is, the more successful he or she will be—and the more secure his or

4. *The Essential Drucker* (Collins, 2003), p. 323.

her job will be. When this happens, we have what we call 'collective entrepreneurship'—or ... 'the team as hero.'"[5]

Show That You Appreciate That Risk-Taking Is Essential to Innovation

- "To innovate, we must take risks. That's tough. I know that [especially in organization an as large as ours,] it's easy to avoid criticism. Just do nothing, say nothing, and be nothing."

If the Innovation Is a Necessary Response to a Problem, Accentuate the Positive

- "Innovation is my theme today and, in that spirit, I want to get away from *we have a problem* and move the discussion forward."

Talk About the Anticipatory Nature of Innovation

True innovations lead the customer or the industry, providing what people didn't know they wanted.

- "The real challenge is to give customers what they *will* want. That's why industry leaders consistently *anticipate* customers' needs ... and translate today's emerging trends into tomorrow's successful products. We have to think like the great hockey player Wayne Gretzky. When they asked him how he managed to lead the league is scoring year after year, Gretzky said this:'I skate to where the puck is going to be, not to where it has been.' And that's what *we've* got to do."

- "Tom Peters says—and I agree—that 'the phrase "out-of-the-box thinking" is far too mellow. It's too limited, and lim-

5. Robert Reich, "Entrepreneurship Reconsidered: The Team as Hero," *Harvard Business Review,* 65, May-June 1987, p. 77.

iting.' Instead, he says, 'it's a matter of breaking completely out of familiar ways of thinking, of not limiting yourself to what is comfortable or comprehensible to you.' Maybe we should give 'out-of-the-box' a rest ... and focus more on Gary Hamel's term 'strategy innovation,' which is 'the ability to reinvent the basis of competition within existing industries and to invent entirely new industries.'[6] To create shareholder value, you have to break the rules. To just continue to do the same thing you're already doing, but a little better—which most people try to do and which they regard as the least risky thing to do—is really the *riskiest* strategy of all! Someone else who has the ingenuity and the courage to break the rules will surpass you."

Add example:

■ "The semiconductor device that replaced the vacuum tube ... was one of the greatest inventions since the wheel. But how many of the top 10 vacuum-tube manufacturers do you think became top-10 semiconductor producers? Answer: zero. They were content where they were and they failed to grasp the opportunities. And new companies took over."

■ "As Bill Walsh, coach of so many winning San Francisco 49ers football teams, put it, 'More than creating, innovation involves anticipating. It is having a broad base of knowledge on your subject and an ability to see where the game is headed.'"[7]

6. "Killer Strategies That Make Shareholders Rich," *Fortune*, June 23, 1997.
7. Quoted by Ray Didinger, *Game Plans for Success* (McGraw-Hill, 1996), p. 178.

- "In a book called *Competing for the Future*,[8] the authors make a very key point: meeting only the articulated needs of clients/customers you *already* serve ... will concede vast opportunities to more farsighted competitors. The real challenge is to give people what they *will* want. That's why we have to *anticipate* the needs of our customers/clients/end users ... and translate today's new trends into tomorrow's successful products."

- "John Gardner, the renowned diplomat and educator, once wrote that 'The future announces itself from afar. But most people are not listening. The noisy clatter of the present drowns out the tentative sounds of things to come.... Leaders who have the wit to perceive and the courage to act will be credited with a gift for prophecy that they do not necessarily have.'[9] In other words: you can see the future—*and* get a lot of credit for it—*if* you know where to look."

Discuss the Importance of an Emphasis on Innovation and New Ideas

- "We must keep the pipeline full of new ideas: new ideas are the basis of innovation. I know how long the lead time between concept and application can be. And I know we can't turn on the spigot and expect something to come out, if we've let the reservoir at the other end run dry."

- "An aggressive new product program creates a climate of energy and growth—a belief that the company has its best years still ahead of it. It raises morale; it contributes, as nothing else can, to a spirited and upbeat organization.

8. Gary Hamel and C.K. Prahalad (Harvard Business School Press, 1994).
9. John W. Gardner, *On Leadership,* reprint edition (Free Press, 1993), p. 131.

And it helps us attract and retain superior people."
- "In today's business environment, just letting it happen isn't good enough. Everybody is trying to understand the marketplace and the consumer better—and to respond faster—than everyone else. Thinking out of the box is not a luxury but a necessity. Intelligent risk-taking is essential. As one consultant [, James Morse,] put it, 'The only sustainable competitive advantage comes from out-innovating the competition.'[10] And that is exactly what we must do."
- "Innovation is a paradox: on the one hand, it can't be forced or 'managed, in the usual sense; on the other hand, we have to stimulate it and create the preconditions for it, all over our company."

Note That You Don't Have to Be an Industry Leader to Innovate
- "An economist [Burton Klein] once examined 50 major American innovations over a period of several decades … and found that *none* of them came from a company that was an industry leader at the time of the innovation!"

Point out That Innovation Can Take Many Forms
- "Innovation doesn't always have to be like a big loud roll of thunder. It can be like a lightning flash—a brilliant insight, a quick and relatively minor change that reconnects with customers/end users/clients in a new and imaginative way."

Talk About the Fun/Play Component of Innovation
- "As we cope with it all, we can't lose our enthusiasm for the

10. James F. Morse, "Predators and Prey: A New Ecology of Competition," *Harvard Business Review*, May/June 1993, p. 75, quoted by Tom Peters, *The Circle of Innovation* (Vintage, 1999), p. 29.

challenges or our sense of fun. Remember that an innovation mentality is a 'fun' or 'play' mentality. And also, there's an important link between enthusiasm and success. Innovation … enjoyment … success. They all tie together in a fundamental way."

Urge the Audience Members to Promote Innovation

Stress what they can do if they develop their communication skills to encourage innovation:

- "New ideas are often not elegant; they're not pretty. It's not immediately clear how they'll work—or even *if* they'll work. They need persuasive energy behind them. They need advocates who can write and speak clearly, concisely, and convincingly. If you really believe you've uncovered a way to do something better … or a new opportunity for our/your company, … you need to be as persuasive as possible to put it across and build support for it."

Close by Charging the Audience with Being Innovative

- "We are where we are today because of the innovation and passion of those who came before us. So I charge you … in fact, I *challenge* you … to be *just* as creative, just as ingenious, just as *bold* … and to deliver the ideas that build on their remarkable legacy … *[maybe add, if appropriate:* and transform our company and the entire industry]."
- "Companies don't innovate; *people* do. If we give our people the stimulation, the tools, and the encouragement, we can be leaders *and* be innovative as well. If we emphasize training and practice, we can keep the new ideas flowing. And if we conscientiously and consistently recognize innovation, we will become what we reward."

Part Five

Ceremonial Speeches (Internal or External)

C eremonial speeches accompany events around which people have certain feelings, partly by virtue of the words that the speaker says. Thus, a good ceremonial speech will clearly interpret the event for the audience. For example, "This is a very special day. We're here to ... *[welcome, commemorate, dedicate, recognize, etc.]*."

36. Introducing Others

If You're Presiding at a Local Business Organization or Economic Forum

- "Today I'm doubly honored and twice blessed. I get to preside once again at this gathering of friends, colleagues, and business leaders of our great city. And I get to welcome to this forum and to our city a very special individual."

Enumerate the Person's Strengths and Illustrate Each with an Example

You should do this in the body of your introduction:

- "*[Strength:]* He's a product guy through and through. *[Example:]* He has a firm grasp and a deep understanding of the innovative design, engineering, technology, and marketing that are going to separate the winners from losers in the year ahead."

If the Person Is Multitalented or Multifaceted

- "*[Name]* has incredible talent and versatility. If he were a major league baseball player, he'd be a starting pitcher who wins 20 games a year … *and* a .300 hitter … *and* a part-time coach with a deep understanding of the fine points of the game."
- "*[Name]* represents that all-too-rare combination of thinker, doer, and leader … *[or whatever combination of talents].*"

Praise the Person's Persistence and Success Orientation

- "She is a leader and a winner, because she knows how to persist and persevere. She doesn't even think of the opposite of success. See, I didn't even use the word. Successful

133

people never do. They may talk of their 'setbacks,' their 'mistakes,' their 'false starts'—all of which lead to learning and experience."

■ "If he believes she's doing the right thing for [company/organization], its people, its customers, its consumers, and its shareholders, he will never, *ever* back down."

Talk About the Person as an Individual

This should come after you review his or her career accomplishments. Lead with:

■ "Just what kind of an individual has been able to accomplish so much?"

Discuss the Person's Values and Pragmatism

■ "He/She lives by a small set of ideas that, taken together, are a forceful, pragmatic crystallization of volumes of practical management wisdom."

Praise the Person's Leadership/Management Skills
Example:

■ "She respects—and tries to surround herself with—really smart people who *also* understand the business, take intelligent risks, and believe in growth."

If the Person Is Genuinely Nice

■ "His/Her management style represents the very best in business leadership." *[You can expand this with examples.]*

If the Person Has Considerable Practical Experience

If you're introducing someone with much experience, you might want to build your introduction around those credentials.

■ "There is absolutely no way I could do justice to [name] by reading his/her résumé out loud. A list of 'degrees earned' and 'positions held' tells you nothing about 'feats accomplished,' 'crises managed,' or 'key leadership skills acquired.' So let me provide you with a few facts in those last three areas."

Close by Summarizing the Person's Strengths

■ "What this all adds up to it that he/she is an energetic, active leader with a clear vision of what he/she wants … and the courage to push—uphill if necessary—to get it done."

For a Government Official

■ "Ladies and gentlemen, our speaker is a person whose intelligence, competence, and dedication to America and its people are a model and an inspiration for all who devote themselves to public service. They are exactly what we hope for … and what we expect from our country's leaders. Please join me, then, in welcoming … *[title and name]*."

For Someone Whose Work Has Had Broad Impact

■ "Ladies and gentlemen, please join me in welcoming someone whom I know we all admire, because her ideas, talents, and plain hard work have done—and continue to do—so very much to contribute to the well-being of *[our nation, community, etc.]* … and to shape its fortunes: *[full name]*."

End the Introduction on a High Note

■ "Ladies and gentlemen, it's both an honor and a pleasure to introduce to you an outstanding *[category to which the person belongs— … leader, athlete, public servant]*. Please join me in welcoming *[title and full name]*."

- "I know you're all as eager as I am to hear what he/she has to say to us, so please welcome … *[name]*!

If You're Introducing an Out-of-Town Visitor to a Local Group, You Can End With

- "Ladies and gentlemen, would you please give a rousing *[name of city]* welcome to *[title and name]*."

37. Welcoming Remarks

Most welcoming speeches, whether at formal conferences or festive events, have two things in common: they are short and they explain why the speaker is happy (or experiencing whatever other emotion is appropriate) and why the audience should be, too. Here are some specific suggestions.

Open with Enthusiasm

■ "This is a great day/evening/etc ... and it's an enormous pleasure for me to be a part of it all."

If the Audience Members Are There Because They've Been Selected

If the members of the audience are there because of some selection process, consider referring to this fact:

Example:

■ "Let me congratulate all of you on being selected for what I hope will be two of the most intense, stimulating, and rewarding weeks *[or whatever the time interval is]* of your professional lives."

If the Event Is Periodic

If the event is held regularly, e.g., annually or quarterly:

■ "It's a pleasure to welcome all of you *[optional: enumerate the kinds of people, e.g. media, guests]* to *[venue/location]* and to the latest edition of this long-running and highly successful show."

Welcome the Audience

Somewhere in your opening, actually welcome the members of the audience:

■ "I just can't tell you what a pleasure it is for me to be here to welcome you to ...."

To Welcome Representatives or Dignitaries from a Foreign Country

■ "*[List the most eminent names],* ... members of *[organization holding the event],* ... and honored guests, I am pleased and privileged to welcome you to *[city].*"

If appropriate, dwell briefly on the similarities between the visitors' land and yours:

■ "I know that many of you have traveled very far to be with us tonight. And yet, I hope that you will feel very much at home here with us in *[city or region].* I hope that you will feel that, in a sense, you have not traveled very far at all! For truly, our two lands have much in common: *[whatever you have in common].*"

If You're Welcoming Them to Any Kind of Reunion

■ "How many of you recall your 10th or 15th or 20th high school reunion? Think back. What was your most powerful impression? I know what *mine* was: I was actually surprised that I still recognized everybody! I don't know what I'd expected—that they'd all have had plastic surgery or something—but I remember thinking, 'They all look the same!' And then I thought, 'My gosh, we're all just grown-up kids!' Well, we are, aren't we? And isn't it fascinating to see *how* we've all grown up? That's what reunions do: they allow us to reconnect; they remind us of our continuity with the past, of our ancestry, of our ties of blood, friendship, and roots. They're a vehicle for the collective remembering of shared experiences."

Other points you can make about reunions:

- "Reunions are a way of introducing *dis*continuity, too, of interrupting the routines of our lives, so that we can return to them refreshed and reinvigorated."

- "Reunions also remind us of the various arrangements and systems of people within which we live, of the many groups to which we belong and the many people with whom we have so much in common and from whom we have so much to learn. In a time when life is all too chaotic and unpredictable, reunions remind us that there is order and structure to our existence, that we live not alone, but within networks of other human beings."

- "Reunions are a way to experience the friendship and kindness of our fellow human beings. They're a time for happiness and laughter, a powerful antidote to the isolation and loneliness that characterize modern life."

- *[End comments on reunions with:]* "And before we get too serious about this, reunions are also a terrific excuse to take a vacation and throw a party. And let us *never* underestimate the importance of taking a vacation and throwing a party!"

End by Welcoming Them Again

- "Thank you all for coming here today/tonight. And again, my warmest welcome to you all."

If entertainment is to follow, close on an anticipatory note:

- "It's going to be an incredible evening! Welcome … and enjoy!!"

38. Tributes and Memorials

Tributes and memorials emphasize individual's personal qualities, as in the phrases below. Your own personal anecdotes, if short and relevant, can be very effective. You may find other ideas in Section 36.

For a Retirement Tribute

- *[At or near the beginning of speech:]* "Thank you all for being here today to help us pay tribute to a man/woman who is leaving our company/organization after ___ years of service."

- *[At or near the ending:]* "Samuel Johnson once advised, 'Do not think of retiring from the world until the world will be sorry that you retire.' Well, *[name]*, we congratulate you on your timing: the world of [company/organization] *is* sorry to see you retire. But your achievements are your legacy, and they are indeed an inspiration to us all. And so we say goodbye fondly … and with the hope that this new period in your life will be full of health, happiness, and contentment."

If the person has served for an extraordinarily long time, you can comment on that.

Example:

- "30 years—just think of it: an entire generation, during which *[name]* has devoted his/her professional life to the growth and success of *[company/organization]*."

Praise the Individual's Energy and Capacity for Hard Work

- "If you think that all of these accomplishments require enormous energy, you're quite right. Mark Twain was once asked the secret of his success and he replied, 'I was born excited.' Those of us who have observed *[name]*'s cheerful personality, his/her many years of worldwide travel, *[insert other qualities as appropriate]*, and his/her prodigious achievements, must conclude that like Twain, he/she was born excited. One simply could not do what he/she has done … without a burning enthusiasm for—and commitment to—hard work."

Praise the Individual's Courage

A good means of praising this virtue is by comparing it to the courage of an eagle:

- "The eagle carried special fascination for the famous American painter and naturalist, James Audubon. It was not just the beauty or the sheer size of this great bird that fascinated Audubon. It was its courage. When storms came and the rest of the bird kingdom sought shelter in the trees, the eagle soared aloft to hunt."

If the Person Is Passionate and Outspoken

- "I could have spent this entire speech talking about the passion of *[name]*. He/She has the energy of a passionate person—an apparently bottomless reserve of it. He/She is passionately outspoken. You never have to wonder what *[name]* thinks best for our company; he/she is right up front with it."

If the Person Is a Proven Motivator

- "He's/She's given his/her people the encouragement and latitude they need in order to excel. He's/She's always stimulating their thinking, always motivating them, always probing and demanding more."

If the Person Is Known for Clear Values and Solid Principles

■ "[Name] is a remarkable human being. Underlying all his/her achievements is the personality of a simple, generous person of rock-solid principles, an individual with the relatively rare ability to identify a goal that's worth pursuing—and then pursue it with bulldog tenacity."

■ "If he/she believes he's/she's doing the right thing for [organization], its people, its customers, its consumers, [add if appropriate: and its shareholders,] he/she will never, ever back down."

If Appropriate, Praise the Person's Thirst for Risk and Innovation

■ "Whatever his/her endeavors, whether as CEO of his/her company, as a spokesperson for American business, or as a concerned citizen, he's/she's constantly searching for new ideas, new insights, and new ways to bring people together in productive enterprise."

■ "[Name] is a true business innovator. He's/She's always challenging his/her people—and himself/herself—to come up with the breakthrough thinking that builds businesses. He's/She's not afraid to take risks and push ahead with promising but unproven ideas."

If the Person Has a Record of Opposing Government Interference

■ He/She will resist, with every fiber of his/her being, attempts by governments to legislate the private behavior of law-abiding citizens."

If the Person Has a Record of Working with Government to Benefit the Organization

■ "In addition to his/her broad grasp of the company, he/she has a deep understanding of the complex relationships between government and commerce. And through his/her personal grace and eloquence, he's/she's built an extensive network of influential contacts—politicians, business people, and community leaders—and leveraged it to contribute to the success of the organization/company."

If Appropriate, Praise the Person's Devotion to His or Her Family

Example:

■ "He has always been a compassionate and caring family man, and this dimension of his life, especially his talented/ charming wife [and son/daughter/children], has no doubt been a great source of support in all that he's achieved."

If Appropriate, Praise the Person's Leadership and/or Management Skills

■ "[Name] is also a superb motivator of people. He/She inspires everyone who works for him/her. And he/she provides the autonomy that enables his/her people to develop their skills … and realize their full potential as business managers and leaders."

■ "His/Her understanding of the business/industry/organization, from both an intellectual and an intuitive point of view, is very strong, and he's/she's adept at finding unconventional, creative solutions."

■ "He/She combines outstanding technical competence with a personal style that people find magnetic. As with all natural leaders, people want to follow him/her."

- "He's/She's a hands-on manager, a strong motivator with a thorough grasp of the business."
- "He's/She's a keen business strategist who practices intelligent, aggressive risk-taking."

Talk about the person's potential for further development:

- "There's no doubt in my mind that even with all that he's/she's accomplished so far, he/she still he has significant untapped management and leadership potential."

Finish by Summarizing the Person's Strengths

- "All in all, he/she is a fine [name of his/her profession/specialty], a consummate professional, an outstanding leader, and an extraordinary human being."

39. Awards Presentations

Your speech should praise the individual for the qualities that won the award. For other suggestions, see Section 38.

Welcome the Audience and Tell Them Why They're There

Example:

- "Good evening! I'm delighted to welcome you to *[name of event]*. We're here tonight to celebrate accomplishments and to recognize leadership. And indeed, there's much to celebrate."

If You Can't Be There in Person (and Are Being Videotaped), Apologize

- "Congratulations and best wishes to our winners! I wish I could be there in person to thank you for your efforts and to wish each one of you the very best."

Consider Starting with a Summary of the Qualities of the Winner(s)

- "Our [first/next/etc.] award tonight goes to a man/woman who is an incredible fountain of innovative ideas, who motivates and develops people like no one I've ever seen, and who has almost single-handedly *[whatever the winner did]*. He/She is ... *[name and title]*." *[Then go into his/her accomplishments.]*
- "Tonight/today/etc. we are recognizing *[name]* for *[summary of qualities that won the award]*."

If an Award Is for Professional Excellence or Achievement

- "James B. Conant, a great educator and president of

Harvard University, once said that 'Each honest calling, each walk of life, has its own elite, its own aristocracy, based on excellence of performance.' Well, today/tonight, we're here to recognize excellent performance in *our* walk of life: ...."

■ "Vince Lombardi, the immortal football coach, once observed that 'the spirit, the will to win, and the will to excel are the things that endure. These qualities are so much more important than the events that occur.' And those are the very qualities that I see in this room tonight."

Convey Your Excitement

A good way to convey excitement is by implying that you could say much more about the person:

■ "This is a *real* pleasure for me. My only regret is that I'm limited to ___ minutes ... because there is *so* much more I could say about the character, the creativity, the business acumen, and the leadership skills of *[first and last names]*. But let me give you the short version."

If the Winner Has Been Underappreciated or Unappreciated

■ "It has *not* been easy, and perhaps he/she hasn't always received the credit, the admiration, the *gratitude* he/she deserves. Tonight we're going to make sure he/she does."

In the Case of Multiple Awards, Express Enthusiasm for Being Among Winners

■ "This evening is a real treat for me: I *love* to be among peak performers and winners like you. There's a certain optimism and energy about them that I can almost feel in the air."

If an Award Is for a Competition or Contest

■ "Today/tonight/etc. we are celebrating a triumph of concentration and endurance. Our contestants have performed flawlessly throughout this competition. They did so because of their long-term concentration and endurance, their truly prodigious investment of themselves in developing their talent. Whenever I hear people say to a musician, 'I'd give anything to be able to play the way you do,' I always think to myself that in reality they probably *wouldn't* make the sacrifice."

If an Award Is Named for Someone

If an award commemorates someone, link the qualities of the winner(s) with those of the person honored.

Example:

■ "Today/Tonight we're honoring an exceptional group of people, all of whom carry on the legacy of *[name]*—a legacy of *[examples of qualities:]* the drive for continual improvement, the concern for the customer, and the creation of the future."

If Presenting an Award to a Group

If, for example, you're presenting awards to science fair winners, you can talk about the qualities that the winners have in common:

■ "Although I don't know each of you personally, I still don't feel like a stranger, because I do know a few things *about* you. And that's because I know a little bit about achievement. I've found that high achievers, in any field, tend to have a lot in common. So let me make some educated guesses." *[Praise their pride of workmanship, courage in the face of failure, willingness to learn, and other virtues.]*

If the Award Recipients Are Artists

- "Congratulations to each of this year's contestants. I hope your talents continue to flourish and grow. And I hope that the creation and enjoyment of art will be a source of pleasure and self-discovery for the rest of your lives."

- "The nature of art is to convey, through line, shape, and color … through sound and movement … the experience and vision of the artist, in a language that is both distinctive and universal. This language in turn broadens our experience and vision, reminding us of our diversities and our commonalities, our past and our future, our challenges and our opportunities. Our winners have enriched us in all of these ways, and we are profoundly grateful."

If an Award Is Coming from Peers

- "Excellence, in its purest form, is most easily recognized by the others in a particular field. So when we hear someone referred to as 'a musician's musician' or 'a ballplayer's ballplayer,' we know that here's a performer who's so good, whose mastery of the technique is so complete, that even his/her peers agree about how good he/she is."

If an Award Is for a Difficult Achievement

- "Despite all the obstacles, he/she/this team remained focused, energized, and deeply committed."

If an Award Is for Community Service or Some Other Commitment

- "Someone[1] once said that 'all the beautiful sentiments in the world weigh less than a single lovely action.' To our honoree(s), let me say that you are people/a person of

1. James Russell Lowell, "Rousseau and the Sentimentalists."

good sentiments *and* good actions, and you've done it all with a strength of commitment and a generosity of spirit that are an inspiration to all of us."

If the Winner(s) Is/Are Eligible for Next Year's Award

- "Continue to do what you've been doing, and you'll be all the more likely to be back here next year ... and be recognized once again for your commitment, your creativity, and your excellence."

If Appropriate, Discuss the Implications of the Winner's/Winners' Accomplishment(s)

Examples:

At the individual level:

- "The skills and initiative on this recognition today, if you develop and nurture them, will be of immense benefit, not only to those with whom you work, but to all of society, for the rest of your life."

For society at large:

- "What we're doing here today is more than an awards ceremony, as enjoyable as that is. By singling out and recognizing this/these winner(s), we send a message that this is the kind of society we want to have—a society that respects individual achievement and takes pride in the values of *[organization] [optional: list the values]*."
- *[Or:]* "—a society of individuals who never stop learning, relish hard work, and direct their creative energies outward as well as inward."

Finish by Congratulating the Winner(s) Once Again

Congratulate the winner(s) and, if appropriate, directly address him/her/them and present the award.

Examples:

- "It's been a great turnaround effort for an important business/division! So thanks and congratulations to … *[name].*"

- *"[Name],* I've admired your leadership and professionalism for *years* now, and I am absolutely delighted to see you recognized in such a prestigious and public way. Congratulations!"

- *"[Name],* my warmest personal congratulations. It's a great pleasure to present you with this *[optional: insert name of award]* award!"

- "Our deepest thanks and warmest congratulations to … *[name].*"

Before Presenting the Award, Consider Briefly Recapping the Winner's Accomplishment(s)

- *"[Name],* for being an outstanding motivator and leader, and for *[insert accomplishment(s)],* I am delighted to present to you with this *[name of award].* Congratulations!"

If Your Speech Is to Be Followed by Activities

- "Let me extend my warmest congratulations to our winner(s) … and once again welcome you all to what I know will be a most enjoyable evening."

40. Remarks for Accepting an Award

Show Appreciation and Humility

- "I've heard that 'the greater the appreciation, the shorter the speech should be.' Well, if that's true, then I should sit down right now!"

- "At moments like this, I recall the advice given by [the former Israeli prime minister] Golda Meir: "Don't be so humble,' she said.'You are not that great.'"

- "This is a very special honor, and I'm truly grateful. Mark Twain once said that he could live for two weeks on a good compliment. At moments like this, I know just what he was talking about."

- "I'm delighted and grateful that you've seen fit to honor me in this way. But you know, you can take yourself too seriously. There's a story about the late, great football coach Vince Lombardi. He was in a restaurant when a little boy came up to his table. Before the boy could say anything, Lombardi took a menu and autographed it for him. The boy wasn't impressed.'I don't want a menu,' he said.'I just wanted to borrow the catsup.' As I say, you have to keep it all in perspective."

If You're Receiving an Honorary Doctorate

- "I understand that if you take the academic route, you can earn a Ph.D. in seven to 10 years. Well, I've been in management for [number] years, and there's so much to learn that sometimes I feel as if I haven't made it to the master's degree, let alone a doctorate. So I'm especially delighted by this recognition, and I accept with pleasure and gratitude."

If You're Receiving an Award for Your Organization, Share the Credit

■ "My accomplishments really aren't mine alone: over the years, I have a lot of help—from our great management team. All that you've given me credit for doing … couldn't have been done without them."

If You're Receiving an Award for Contributing to a Cause, Share the Credit

■ "I'm pleased to accept this honor, on behalf of *[company]* and—much more importantly—on behalf of the *[company]* people who have headed up chapters, who have worked on projects, and who have really embodied the mission of this organization." *[You can continue with* "In the next few minutes, I want to focus on them."*]*

■ "On behalf of all of us at *[company/organization]*, I'm delighted and honored to accept this award." *[Consider continuing with:]* "I'm reminded of the young mother who was explaining the Golden Rule to her six-year-old. She ended up by saying, 'Always remember that we're in this world to help others.' The child pondered this for a minute—and then asked, 'Well, what are the others here for?' We all know the answer: the others are here to help us. So that's why I accept this award—not only for myself, but on behalf of everyone else—the 'others' … who really made it all happen."

■ "I'm very grateful for this recognition. But there are many others who should also be acknowledged today. So I accept this award on behalf—and in appreciation—of the many thousands of people who have responded to the call of their conscience … and who, through their monetary support and their everyday behavior at home and on the job, have furthered the cause of … *[cause]*."

Another Possibility: Refocus Attention from Yourself to the Organization

■ "But really, I should be the one [*or, if accepting on behalf of your organization,* we should be the ones] honoring *you* … and giving *you* an award. It's *you*—and all the people you help—who are the real winners today/tonight. It's a privilege for me/us just to be able to help make your work possible. To receive an award for doing *that* is to be doubly honored."

If Appropriate, Share Credit with Your Spouse and/or Other Family Member(s)

If you acknowledge family members, keep the list short.

Example:

■ "The qualities you're honoring me for today … are partly the result of the influence of my husband/wife/partner of __ years. His/her encouragement, counsel, support, and appreciation of what I've become have been powerful positive forces in my life."

If You're Receiving an Award for Career Accomplishments

■ "The usual symbol for career progress is a ladder. But I think mountain climbing is a more appropriate metaphor. On a ladder, the rungs are evenly spaced and the whole thing generally leans against a flat, even surface. Making your way up involves little more than lifting one foot over another. But climbing a mountain, like pursuing a career, involves many skills that have nothing to do with climbing a ladder—and many dangers. A mountain is rough and steep. Your footing is often uncertain and, almost inevitably, you will suffer scrapes and falls. You sometimes have to go down a little in order to go up. And the higher you go, the farther you can see and the more exhilarated you feel—and the greater the risk if you stumble."

If the Award Is Coming from a Group of Your Peers

- "To me, being chosen for the *[name of award]* is like receiving an Oscar or a Tony: it represents the acclaim of your peers, of people best qualified to judge your performance. And that's why I consider it the highest accolade that any of us can receive."

If the Award Is for Community Service

- "In the words of an old proverb, ' Honor the tree that shelters you.' We're all responsible for sustaining our communities. We're all obligated to support the institutions—social, cultural, and intellectual—on which our communities depend. We all have to give something back, in proportion to our resources, our influence, and our ability. That's what it means to be a member of the community. That's what I've tried to do—and I'm delighted that you've seen fit to recognize me for my efforts."

Accept and End by Thanking the Awarding Organization Again

If it's appropriate, you may want to share credit:

- "I thank you once again for this award, and I accept it with pleasure, and with full credit to all the people—parents, teachers, coaches, and mentors of all kinds—who over the years have shaped my values and made me worthy of your recognition."

- "I'm pleased to accept, not only for myself, but also on behalf of all of our many *[company]* people, who are working unselfishly to make their communities better places in which to live."

- "Again, my/our thanks to *[awarding organization]* for recognizing me/us in this most gratifying way."

- "On behalf of all of us at *[company]*, thank you once again for this great honor."

- "Thank you once again for your kind words and good wishes."

- "Thank you again for this award. I'll continue to do all I can do deserve it."

- "Thank you again. I'm delighted that you've chosen to honor me in this way."

- "Let me close by thanking you once again for this honor … and wishing you a future that's even more successful than your past. Your mission is important and I'm proud to help you fulfill it."

41. Milestones and Other Dedications

Emphasize Immediately That You Recognize the Significance of the Event

- "Good morning/afternoon/etc. and thank you for inviting me to be part of this important occasion."
- "We're here today to commemorate ...."

If something is being dedicated to an individual, you can commemorate his/her qualities.

Example:

- "We gather here today to commemorate the dreams, the vision, and the hard work of ... [name]."

Credit and Congratulate the People Who Made the Event Possible

At a plant startup, for example, you would probably credit and congratulate the employees.

- "Today is a very special day for me, for our company, and most especially for you. Without question, today belongs to you. We're doing more than celebrating a successful start of the plant, as important as that is. When I look at this facility—and what you've been able to accomplish in only [time interval], I see the future of our company. Everything we're trying to achieve is brought together in one place— and working beautifully!"

Dedicate

- "So today, [date], we dedicate this [building, etc.] to ...."

Finish with Appreciation and Congratulations

- "Thank you for inviting me ... and congratulations to all of you."

42. Christmas/Holiday Gatherings

There are many ways to link the numerous themes of Christmas and other winter holidays with the culture of your organization and with your business. Here are a few suggestions.

Draw Parallels Between Workplace Family and Individual Families

- "The holiday season is a time for celebrating our connections with our fellow human beings, especially our various families—the families consisting of parents, siblings, spouses or partners, children … and our on-the-job family, the people with whom we spend so much time. There are, it seems to me, some similarities between the two."

- "For one thing, you can't pick your relatives—and you generally don't have much control over the people with whom you work, either!"

- "Second—and more important—each family, regardless of who its members are, will be strong and successful *if* those members are honest and trusting … and *if* they work for the common good and maintain respect for the individual."

- "What does a healthy family like ours do when it's challenged as we are? Well, it adapts. The various members work to complement each other's strengths and to give support where it's needed. Everybody focuses his or her problem-solving skills on creating new goals, new solutions, and new answers. Everybody works together with a fresh commonality of purpose. Finally, a healthy family like ours responds to challenge with realism about its strengths, optimism about the future, and a good-natured sense of perspective, goodwill, and even fun."

Finish with the following or some variation of it:

- "God bless all of you, and all of *your* families as well, with the most joyous of holiday seasons … and with an abundance of happiness and health in the new year."

Talk About the Sensory Experience of Christmas

- "The thing that strikes me about Christmas is that it's such a total experience. For a few weeks, our whole environment is transformed. There are the lights, of course, lifting us out of winter's cold and gloom, just as they've done for many centuries, and reminding us of the warmth of human companionship and of the spring that's never far behind. But there's so much more … because Christmas captures *all* of our senses. We listen for jingle bells in the country … and for silver bells in the city. We smell the pine needles on the tree and the turkey on the table. We even *dream* of a white Christmas, in the hope that nature will accommodate our longing for a total experience. And that's just the English and American version. Everywhere that people celebrate this marvelous holiday, you'll find the special foods, costumes, songs, and decorations that create the total Christmas environment."

Talk About the General Goodness of the Season

- "Here's an observation by a leading authority on Christmas—Charles Dickens:' I have always thought of Christmas time as a good time; a kind, forgiving, charitable, pleasant time; the only time I know of, in the long calendar of the year, when men and women seem by one consent to open their shut-up hearts freely.… And therefore,… though it has never put a scrap of gold or silver in my pocket, I believe that it has done me good, and will do me good; and I say, "God bless it."' Well, Mr. Dickens, I couldn't agree more! So God bless Christmas—and God bless all of you!"

Talk About the Holiday Season as a Time of Hope

- "This holiday season is a time of hope. Our ancestors hoped that by lighting lights, they could brighten the winter gloom and hasten the coming of spring. The story of Christmas offers the hope of salvation for all humanity. And throughout the holiday season, we all try to behave with an extra measure of generosity, kindness, and joy. We show that we *can* love our fellow human beings and promote peace on earth just as the great teachers, saints, and prophets down through the ages have always urged us to do. And doing all of that gives us hope that things will get better, because indeed we can make *them* better, not only during the holiday season, but all year round."

- "For thousands of years, people in many lands have been holding Festivals of Light in the middle of winter … to express their hope that light and life would return in the spring. And in that spirit *we* are confident and optimistic that next year will be better because of all that we've done—and *will* do—to make it better. Thank you all for being here today/tonight. I hope that your holiday season is full of warmth and joy … and that the New Year brings you health, happiness, and fulfillment of all your hopes."

Part Six

Phrases and Language Strategies for Specific Audiences

43. Audiences Who Do Not Speak English as a First Language

The continuing expansion of English around the globe means that you'll be communicating with more and more new English speakers from traditionally non-English-speaking countries and regions. Because of the number of new speakers and the worldwide cultural prominence of English, there are many situations where misinterpretation can take place.

As you'll see, some of my examples have *more* than one potential communication problem; this situation is not unusual. Unless you are very sensitive to language, it's almost impossible to preclude them all.

The good news is that only eight writing and editing principles will cover a very large number of cases and considerably reduce the burden on the non-native reader/listener.

Use Familiar Words

Replace business and technical jargon—and, in fact, *all* words and meanings whose use is confined to a particular group—with more familiar, everyday words.[1]

instead of using:	consider:
win-win	mutually agreeable
to buy in	to consent to/agree to
to benchmark	to compare
to champion	to advocate
to (dis)incent	to discourage/encourage
issue	problem/obstacle
to leverage	to use, take advantage of

1. Check your thesaurus for alternatives to my alternatives.

instead of using:	consider:
give 110%	*make an extraordinary effort*
executing against[2] our strategies	*implementing/carrying out our strategies*
up to speed	*aware of current development(s)*
a watch-out, a heads-up	*an advance warning*
pushback	*resistance, objections*
across[3] the company	*throughout/everywhere in the company*
deliverables	*accomplishments/(tangible) results*

Avoid Ambiguity

Be sensitive to words with multiple meanings or a wide range of meanings. If a word could be interpreted in various ways, choose another word with a narrower range of meaning. Here are some examples:

- The most obvious sign that our *drive* on the issue is *flagging* is …
  Replace *drive* with *enthusiasm*. Replace *flagging* with *waning* or *declining*.

- Consumers and corporate IT departments *are revolting*. They don't want any more features in Word.
  Replace *revolting* with *in revolt* or *protesting*.

- CEOs are managers of increasingly complex organizations acting according to incentives that are *fairly* proscribed.

2. This meaning of *against* does not occur in conversational speech.
3. The reason for the substitution is that this word has another, distinct meaning: "about as far away as something can be (within the company)."

Replace *fairly* with *substantially* or *essentially* or *somewhat*, to avoid confusion with the other meaning, 'justly.'

■ … changing their *look* …
Replace *look* with *appearance*.

■ *If* one *buys* the arguments of historians …
Replace *buys* with *accepts*.

Use Abstract Words for Abstract Things

Avoid Figurative Language: Although figurative language can be very effective in many contexts, it can also cause problems. For people who might take the words literally, eliminate metaphors.

■ *A deeper look* makes clear that …
Revise to *Greater/longer attention will reveal that* …

■ Some *grumbled* that the plan was assembled hastily …
Replace *grumbled* with *complained*.

■ Especially symbolic of the back-to-basics approach is the decision to *shed* Stephens, a *swaggering* pioneer in technology investment banking.
Replace *shed* with *fire* or (for people who have learned British English) *dismiss*. Replace *swaggering* with *audacious*.

■ … the people *devastated* by news of his current perils …
Replace *devastated* with *who were severely disappointed or upset*.

Avoid Idioms

Replace idioms with phrases whose elements signal the actual meaning. An idiom is a phrase that must be understood *as a whole*; the individual elements provide little or no clue as to the meaning of the whole. Many colloquial and slang expressions are idiomatic.

In *Star Trek IV*, for example, Kirk says to Spock, "If we play our cards right, she'll tell us." Spock replies, "How will playing cards help?" Clearly, Vulcans are not only completely rational and truthful, they're completely literal.

instead of using:	use:
shell out	pay
licking his chops	gloating
get off the ground	enjoy a successful start/ start-up/beginning
push the envelope	test the limits
get a taste of their own medicine	endure what they inflicted on others
shoot themselves in the foot	harm themselves

Increase Clarity by Inserting Implied Words

We often omit words that we consider understood and therefore unnecessary. However, sometimes it's a good idea not to assume. Look for opportunities to make your communication clearer by restoring one or more deleted or implied words, even if the result is a little redundant.

In the examples below, I've inserted words [in brackets] to make the original statements easier to understand.

■ For the 89-year-old, 28,000-employee firm—which *long [for a long time]* set standards in the accounting industry—options are fast dwindling.

■ That's just a sample of the obstacles Wynton Marsalis faces *getting [as he gets/tries to get]* jazz into the ears of today's youth.

■ … to allow foreigners *[who are] living illegally* in the United States to …

- *If [we were]* prudent, we would prepare for this unforeseeable future.

- The sippy cup is the toddler's equivalent of the cell phone, *[and it is]* essential equipment for the kid on the go.

- A 15-story mosque is nearing completion, *[and it is]* the most lavish *[one/mosque]* ever built here.

Reduce the Complexity Caused by Nominalization

When we use nouns instead of verbs or adjectives—a process called "nominalization"—to compress part of a statement, we make communication more complex.

Here's an example:

The expectation of management is that the economy is at the beginning of a recovery.

In other words:

Management expects the economy to begin to recover.

The problem is that each nominalization requires the listener to reconstruct the sentence that's been compressed.

There's another problem, a cultural one: frequent nominalization is well established in the language of bureaucracies, scientists, and others whose professions require an impersonal style of communication. Since actions expressed as nouns rather than verbs allow the agent (the doer) to be omitted, nominalization may leave doubt as to who's doing what. (In fact, bureaucrats may love nominalization just *because* it avoids mentioning who did what.)

To make your communication more conversational and more intelligible to non-native speakers, convert each nominalization to a full sentence.

The following is from the chairman's letter at a corporate Web site. It contains eight (and perhaps nine) nominalizations. Let's rewrite it to eliminate them all. You'll have to break up this long sentence into shorter ones. You may also have to insert and substitute words. Just don't change the meaning.

> *Shareholders will recall that, in pursuit of **recognition** of what we believe to be the underlying value of our assets, management has pursued a series of steps, including the **disposition** of large asset groups at advantageous prices and the **retrenchment** to our strongest and most valuable assets, the **elimination** of current loans and, in **response** to recent conditions, the **imposition** of even more rigorous operating efficiencies than usual, and the **accumulation** of cash to effect a drastic **reduction** in our long-term debt.*

I'll get you started:

> *Shareholders will recall that **as we seek to convince others to recognize** what we believe to be the underlying value of our assets, we have taken several steps. **We have disposed of** large asset groups at advantageous prices. **We have retrenched**[4] our strongest and most valuable assets. **We have eliminated** current loans …*

Avoid Front-Loaded Sentences

Front-loaded sentences have a great deal of subject matter at the beginning, such that the reader/listener has to assemble it all into a single grammatical unit in order to understand the entire sentence. Avoid front-loaded sentences in order to avoid burdening your audience's temporary memory.

Not this:

> *Partnering with leading wine-makers in California, France, and Australia and directing a quality renaissance at their*

4. Whatever that means.

winery, they are emerging as major wine producers.

But this:

They're partnering with leading wine-makers in California, France, and Australia and directing a quality renaissance at their winery. And they're emerging as major wine producers.

Avoid Inverted Sentences and Word Sequences

Instead of these:

- *More worrisome than these practical outcomes, though, is a philosophical problem.*
- *Especially symbolic of the back-to-basics approach is the decision to …*
- *The 10-ton pointy-horned triceratops that roamed North America more than 56 million years ago evolved from dinosaurs not much larger than a house cat, newly discovered fossils of a small dinosaur suggest.*

Use these:

- *However, there is a philosophical problem that is more worrisome than these practical outcomes.*
- *The decision to … is especially symbolic of the back-to-basics approach.*
- *Newly discovered fossils of a small dinosaur suggest that the 10-ton pointy-horned triceratops that roamed North America more than 56 million years ago evolved from dinosaurs not much larger than a house cat.*

Similarly,

As the industry's slump lingers, newspapers large and small [revise to: large and small newspapers] are cutting back or eliminating the listings, which have been a staple of news pages for a century.

To be understood around the world, we must assume that our listeners lack complete access to our rich storehouse of idioms and shorthand expressions, as well as our sensitivity to multiple meanings. Indeed, since non-native speakers are developing new varieties of English around the world, they probably have their own distinctive idioms and abbreviations! So when communicating with international audiences, we must try to uncover hidden implications and ambiguities at every level of language: word, phrase, idiom, and sentence.

44. Employees

The foremost fact in most employees' lives is the absolute power of the organizational hierarchy and of their boss in particular. No matter what the context or event, this fact will be on their minds when they're receiving any executive communication.

Accordingly, authenticity is crucial. (See Part One.) I urge you to review carefully every scripted word you say, every e-mail you send out, and every other communication to those over whom you have control. Purge the documents of corporate jargon, buzzwords, unnecessary acronyms, and inappropriate euphemisms, such as "downsizing" or "rightsizing" or "reduction in force (RIF)" or "headcount adjustment."

No matter what the content of your speech, make sure that you sincerely connect with the audience by using one or more of the strategies described above in Part One and by communicating in clear, simple, familiar language that sounds like you. (See Section 46.)

Again, review everything that's going to go out over your name. How you say it is just important as what you say.

Beyond sincerity, authenticity, and the personal element, here are some specific suggestions for communications to employees.

Cultivate Sensitivity to Pronouns

How you talk about something can reveal the way you see something—*and* influence the way others see it. This principle is evident in the way we use certain pronouns. Therefore:

- Use the pronoun *we*—not your organization's name—whenever you refer to the organization or talk about any activity that involves all employees, including you.

- Don't refer to top management as "we"—you'll only reinforce status distinctions. If you're communicating a strategy decision or change in direction to lower-level employees, refer to the actual executives and staff members who made the recommendation. It's important that there be real people behind top-management decisions.

- Use the pronoun *you* very carefully; it can be highly positive or negative. Sentences framed in terms of *you* can be effective ways to congratulate, include, address, and otherwise connect with the audience. However, always avoid using *you* with anything negative, lest it be taken as accusatory. You probably wouldn't do this intentionally, but it's quite easy to slip into it when you're changing from positive to negative. Be sure to change pronouns, as I changed from *you* to *we* in the following:

  "I think you've done a *great* job. But I know that there's more waste and inefficiency that we can root out. I know we can improve processes, clarify roles, and find smarter ways to do things. I always know we can do better."

If You're New to Your Management/Leadership Position

If you're new to your position, you might want to help employees get acquainted with you by simplifying what you stand for.

Example:

"I think those of you who know me know that all I ask is *[describe whatever you value most]*."

If There Has Been Serious or Disruptive Change

Try to make serious or disruptive change seem less threatening. The next four subsections suggest ways to do so.

CAUTIONARY NOTE: *Consider these alternatives* only *if things are going fairly well. If they're not, you don't want to look as if you're whitewashing a bad situation; you might do more harm than good.*

Make a Statement About the Unavoidability of Change

- "Long ago, a very wise man[5] observed that you can't put your foot in the same river twice, because from one moment to the next, the water moves along and the river is different. He was so right. And not just about rivers. You and I don't come to work in the same company from one month to the next—and probably not even from one *day* to the next!"

If Appropriate, Provide Assurance That the Worst Is Over

- "We're now seeing that it's all been worth the effort. If you've ever put yourself through any kind of fitness program, you know what I'm talking about. First there's pain, then there's gain. [Let me tell you about some of the gains.]"

Note the Connection Between Change and Opportunity

- "Change is something we welcome. It opens up new possibilities; it gives us new opportunities to create competitive advantage ... and achieve the growth we need [and that our shareholders expect of us]. What can we do to take advantage of everything that's going on out there in the

5. The Greek philosopher Heraclitus (6th century BCE).

world outside *[organization]*? How can *we* be the best at turning change into opportunities that create a competitive edge for our company?" *[This can be the subject for the entire speech.]*

Note the Connection Between Change and Renewal

■ "In Greek mythology, there was a god named Proteus. He triumphed over all his challenges by changing his shape. And when *we* respond to *our* challenges, we reinvent ourselves—and our company. We change, as individuals and as an organization, to become better, faster, smarter, stronger. Each success lays the foundation for the next one."

After Talking About the Organization's Success, Give the Employees Credit

■ "I want to thank you all—very, very much. You and your fellow employees have made it all happen. Your skill, your talent, and your commitment have made us as good as we are—and they're going to make us even better."

■ "The future of our company is in your hands. The future never just happens. It's created, sometimes by accident, usually by people acting consciously and seizing—and creating—opportunities. Look what you've accomplished already. You did it not by resisting change, but by welcoming it and managing it."

Ask for Their Ideas

■ "You know, *good* ideas ... are not necessarily *big* ideas. Often there's no telling how big the impact will be. If you turn the rudder of a big ship only a degree or two, you can alter the destination by hundreds of miles. Even a modest innovation can be translated into enormous sales or productivity savings. All of you have good ideas. You just have to challenge yourself to think creatively. You have to constantly be asking yourself questions like 'How can do we do this faster, smarter, better?' *[Consider adding:]* And don't think that every idea has to hit the bull's-eye. Albert Einstein once said, 'How do I work? I grope.' He admitted, 'I think and think for months and years. Ninety-nine times, the conclusion is false. The hundredth time I am right.' You see, the key is to *generate* the 99 ideas, to keep your mind in a state of active curiosity."

Note That Teamwork and Individuality Are Compatible

- "In the world of teamwork, there's plenty of room for individuality. In fact, you can't have good team results without 100% of everyone's ideas and everyone's efforts."

45. Male Addressing Primarily Female Audience: Gender Sensitivity

Here's how a great many people—mostly adherents of political correctness and none of them, I dare say, linguists— think about language and its supposed effect on thought: if we go on using words like *mankind* and *policeman* (and, for some extremists, *history* and *woman*) and sentences like *A dentist might use the new technique on his patient,* then we will in effect be continuing the long-standing prejudices against women that have become embedded in the language.

I don't know whether this argument is true or not. I don't know what goes on in people's heads while they're using particular pronouns and word roots.

But what's important for our purposes is the fact that most literate people now regard it as true. So if you don't use gender-neutral language, you might offend your audience, especially if they are mostly or all female. But stick to the following principles, and you'll be all right:

- If you're speaking about people generally, avoid *man* and all words that contain it and imply only "male." Instead of *mankind,* use *people* or *humanity* (some hardliners won't even let you get by with that because it has *man* in it) or *men and women;* instead of *businessman,* use *(business) executive* or *manager* (or *account executive,* or whatever job title applies); instead of *Congressman,* use *Representative, Senator, Congressperson,* or *Congressional Representative.*

- Avoid using *he/his/him* to point back to an indefinite word or phrase earlier in the sentence. The neatest way to do this is to make the earlier indefinite word or phrase into a plural—that is, add *-(e)s* for a "more than one" meaning;

then you can use *they/their/them*: *Educators might use the new video in **their** classes.*

To point back to an indefinite *everybody/somebody/anybody*, use *him or her*, *him/her*, *his or her*, *his/her* (with the slash-mark), or *a(n)*. *They/their/them* is usually OK, except in formal, impersonal communications.

- Gender-marked: *Everybody got his bonus.*
- Neutral: *Everybody got a bonus.*
- Informal: *Everybody got their bonus.*

Avoid using *she/her* to refer to words that denote traditionally female occupations. Again, the double pronoun may be intolerably awkward, and you may have to rewrite:

- Gender-marked: *Give this to one of the administrators. She'll type it.*
- Neutral (formal): *Give this to one of the administrators, who will type it.*
- Neutral (informal): *Give this to one of the administrators. They'll type it.*
- Neutral (better): *If you want this typed, give it to one of the administrators.*

Gender Sensitivity: Overcompensating

Some speakers and writers like to flaunt their gender sensitivity by using *she* and *her* to refer to an indefinite word earlier in the sentence, even though there's no reason to believe that the person in question is female, e.g., *A doctor might use the new drug on **her** patients.* This usage can also be a signal of in-group membership, whether that group is all women or women plus men who sympathize with their political point of view and are thus defenders of politically correct language (e.g., academics).

Such audiences will probably be impressed with the ostentatious indefinite *her*. On the other hand, if your listeners don't care about this sort of thing, they'll more likely be confused, since no one who is obviously female has been referred to earlier in the sentence.

In my discussions and example phrases, I've used several alternatives. You can determine which sounds best to you.

Part Seven

Becoming a More
Effective Executive Speaker

Part Seven

46. How to Make Your Speech Sound Conversational and Personal

On several occasions I've mentioned the difference between the personal conversational style of most speeches (and personal e-mails) and the impersonal style of legal documents, scientific and technical writing, financial reports, and institutions speaking as institutions. The impersonal style reinforces status differences and you should not use it when you want to speak person to person.

In this section I'll show you some of the linguistic choices that will create a personal style.

Replace *Abstraction* with *Action*

Notice how this option—the second in each pair of sentences—mentions people, as opposed to abstractions.

- a. *The modernization of our facilities is proceeding on schedule.*
- b. *We're modernizing our facilities and proceeding on schedule.*

- a. *Current projections show a very constrained outlook.*
- b. *We are/Our staff is currently projecting a very constrained outlook.*

- a. *Management recommended radical cost reductions.*
- b. *Management recommended that we cut our costs radically.*

- a. *Any increase in the gasoline tax of sufficient size to significantly impact the budget deficit ...*
- b. *If we/the government increase(s) the gasoline tax enough to significantly impact the budget deficit ...*

Replace *Passive* with *Active* Expressions

As above, you have to say who's performing the action, so the resulting style will sound more personal.[1]

- a. *Three thousand additional employees were hired.*
- b. *We/The firm hired three thousand additional employees.*

- a. *Our cost-reduction efforts were intensified.*
- b. *We intensified our cost-reduction efforts.*

- a. *These conclusions, which were drawn from the study, ...*
- b. *These conclusions, which I/we/our consultants drew from the study ...*

- a. *When combined with renewed emphasis on product quality, these efforts can ...*
- b. *When we combine them with renewed emphasis on product quality, these efforts can ...*

- a. *It is assumed that new products will claim a significant market share.*
- b. *We/I assume that the new products will claim a significant market share.*

Break up Long Compound Structures

Insert all the words that are necessary for the revised version to make sense. Examples:

- a. *sales tax increase*
- b. *increase* in *the tax* on *sales*

- a. *user call placement procedure*
- b. *procedure that people use to place calls*

1. Don't avoid the passive completely. If whoever or whatever is performing the action is unknown or irrelevant—perhaps because the audience already knows who or what it is—then the passive expression will work fine.

- a. *committee meeting agenda*
- b. *agenda* for *the meeting* of *the committee*

Impersonal speech and writing—the language of contracts, institutional pronouncements, professional/ technical writing, and other communications in which the parties are not known to each other—is full of these strings: compounds of three, four, and more members are not unusual. One reason is that for specialists communicating with each other, long compounds become a kind of in-group shorthand. Speakers and writers don't have to spell out the relationships between the elements, as I just did, because the audience already knows what they are.

In the official language of institutions, the purpose of these long strings is less functional and more ornamental: people use them because they make communication sound more impersonal (and perhaps, by association with scientific and technical writing, more "professional" or "precise").

When you cultivate a personal style, on the other hand, you're replicating spontaneous speech. You use only those compounds that are clearly understandable; in other words, audiences already know the relationships between the parts and thus regard them as single words, as with *house arrest* and *cat food*. Break up and rearrange any compounds that your audience may not understand readily; spell out their relationships with extra words, as in the examples above.

Expand Nominalized Sentences into Full Sentences
See Section 43, "Reduce the Complexity Caused by Nominalization."

Use Contractions
These two-word blends are a very strong signal of a personal,

conversational style. Here are two categories, with my rec-ommendations for usage.

Category 1: Acceptable for All but the Most Formal/Impersonal Speeches

- Contractions with *not*: *won't, wouldn't, shouldn't, can't, couldn't* (*Mightn't* and *oughtn't* belong here, too, but I don't use them. If they sound OK to you, go ahead and use them.)

- Contractions with pronoun or *that* with *am/are/is*: *I'm, you're, he's, she's, it's, we're, they're, that's*

- Contractions with *will*: *I'll, you'll, he'll, she'll, we'll, they'll*

- Contractions with *have/has*: *I've, you've, he's, she's, it's, they've*

- Contraction of *I would*: *I'd*

Category 2: Acceptable Only in Spoken Language or the Most Informal Written Communications

- Contractions with *is*

These involve all words other than *that* and pronouns, e.g., *Maxine's* ([= Maxine is] *writing the letter*), *executive's* (as in *the executive's leaving.*).

- Contraction of *it will*: *it'll*
- Contraction of pronoun (except *I*) + *would*: *you'd, he'd, she'd, we'd, they'd*
- Contractions of pronoun + *had*: *I'd, you'd, he'd, she'd, they'd*

There are many other contractions in spoken English, and I could've (= could have) named them all. But those are about all that you'll want to use in your everyday speeches.

Personal or Impersonal? How to Choose Your Style

While most of your speeches will be in a personal style, you'll want to be sensitive to those situations in which a little more formality is required—for example, a eulogy or a serious business or scientific/technical presentation. Ask yourself how your subject is typically discussed and what your audience expects. Then adjust your language accordingly.

The above four principles show you how to make your writing sound like conversational speech: just pick the personal form every time. But sometimes you want your speech to be a little more formal, less conversational. To create a style that's in between, apply one or more of the principles to get the effect you want. To go from impersonal to personal, I'd start with #4, then add #1, and then the others.

47. The Most Persuasive Words in the Language

Early in our lives we were taught the importance of "please," "thank you," and other forms of politeness in getting others to do what we want. Throughout this book I've given you numerous other suggestions for being more persuasive by bonding and ingratiating yourself with the audience.

But the persuasive words that I'm about to show you go way beyond politeness. They subtly influence the way the audience sees reality—so once you're conscious of their power, you must use them ethically and with good judgment. (See advice below.)

These words are very common; in fact, they're right in front of your nose. You've probably used them a dozen times already today to get your listeners to accept *your* view of the world as the way things really are, but you're hardly aware that you're doing it. And that's the impact of what I call *push-words*—the most persuasive words in the language.

The first four—

- *true, truly, truth*
- *fact, factual, in (point of) fact*
- *real, really, realize*
- *actual, actually*

—put the speaker's stamp of approval on his/her characterizations of reality. In effect: "My words are telling it like it is."

"Like it is" is the suspect phrase. We all see reality from an individual perspective, but the push-words imply an objective reality of which the listener was, perhaps until this moment, not aware. We're saying, "My picture of the world, as painted by the words I use, is the true one."

Note the way I used "*in fact,* they're right in front of your nose" and "the way things *really* are" a couple of sentences back. It probably went right by you. One reason is that my status as an expert gives my use of "real" and "fact" some weight and credibility. More on this momentarily.

Here's another category: *clear(ly), evident(ly), obvious(ly)*. These push-words reinforce the writer's observations or conclusions. They say, "This is clear to me—and therefore to any other intelligent, right-thinking person." Obviously (get it?), they're subject to misuse by someone whose statements aren't backed by hard evidence or solid reasoning processes.

Finally, we have *practically, virtually, basically,* and *essentially*. The message here is "If there's any way in which the words I used seem not to apply to the reality, it's irrelevant; it doesn't matter." Observe a few cases of *virtually, practically,* or *basically* in action and you'll see how neatly speakers and writers use them to slide past situations in which someone else might call them on the accuracy or appropriateness of the words they've used.

The Power of Push

From long years of observation, I've concluded that most people are not aware of the persuasive power of push-words—or of how blithely and frequently they call upon them. They sincerely believe that their facts are *the* facts.

But serious observers of language know that when it comes to the matchup of words with reality, there's very little in the external world, other than the totally mundane, that we can agree on. And many people also experience a subjective reality that is completely inaccessible to others.

Our ability to use different words for the same thing is a

two-edged sword. It certainly increases our ability to express ourselves. But all too often we get locked into a disagreement about labels—about how a thing or event (including a subjective or mental event) should be *correctly* or *accurately* named or otherwise characterized in words. Such disagreement can be very disruptive. It's one of the roots of most political, religious, ethnic, and ideological conflicts.

Politicians and clerics love to exploit it. Recall such famous Presidential declarations as Nixon's "I am not a crook" and Clinton's "I never had sexual relations with that woman," where the validity of the statements hinged upon differing interpretations of *crook* and *sexual relations*.

You can imagine how effective these push-words can be when used consciously. And the more you use them, the harder you're pushing.

To use push-words effectively and ethically—as politicians, advertisers, and others seldom do—is to be firmly grounded in your own truth. Use the push-words when you can stand unimpeachably by your statements, when their relationship to reality is a matter of conviction and personal truth by virtue of your expertise, experience, or some other, equally valid criterion.

Don't use *fact*, *real*, and the other push-words when you're painting word-pictures of imaginary reality that you want the audience to accept. It's fine to talk about hope, ideals, and dreams (as many of my examples do)—as long as you've made your listeners aware that this is what you're doing.

There is a special name for what is created when a speaker or writer presents hopes, visions, or arbitrary, non-fact-based, wishful-thinking-motivated characterizations as facts: bulls__t.

Congratulations! Now that you have a little insight into the relationship between words and the world they symbolize, you understand more about the practical use of language than at least 90% of your fellow English speakers. And there's a whole lot more to know.

Given the relativity of reality and the imprecision of language, it's easy to see what a philosophical quagmire awaits anyone who tries to explain what we really (there it is again!) mean when we use words like *fact* and *true*. But the guidelines I just gave you should help in most practical situations. Use—don't abuse.

48. How (Not) to Use PowerPoint

Perhaps no piece of software is as universally loved and hated as Microsoft PowerPoint®. Organizations seem addicted to it in the medical sense of the word: "I know it's bad for me, but I can't stop." Many people feel that PowerPoint somehow obstructs communication and understanding, but their organizations insist on it and the sense of expectation is so strong that no one dares defy it.

Let's break down the PowerPoint mystique one piece at a time.

The inability of PowerPoint to convey any but the simplest information has been convincingly argued and well documented.[2] PowerPoint has only a few kinds of information hierarchies (mostly category and subcategory) and is relentlessly linear. These are not the kinds of thinking and information-organizing limitations we should want to impose on ourselves.

I'm fortunate. I learned to think the old-fashioned way—by reading a lot of books and articles that not only examined subjects from many points of view, but also developed ideas in many different ways. This kind of input is the exact opposite of PowerPoint, which, if used as a thinking tool, can be exceedingly limiting.

Another item in the indictment: PowerPoint's many options for ornamentation—so many ways to jazz up presentations, waste people's time, and contribute nothing to understanding.

But to me, the strongest objection to obligatory and

2. See *The Cognitive Style of PowerPoint* by Edward R. Tufte (Graphics Press, 2003), www.edwardtufte.com.

over-intrusive PowerPoint—the one that makes it repulsive to me as a speaker—is that once again technology has trumped humanity. What's going on to the right of the bullets or within the starburst that explodes to reveal the next graphic is made far more interesting than what's going on behind the lectern.

Elaborate, attention-grabbing visuals undermine the unique power of a speech as one of the few human-to-human communication forms that we have left. And, as comedian Louie Anderson used to say, that's just not right.

If the speaker has decided to show on the screen an exact or near-exact copy of the words he or she is reading, insult is added to injury. The speaker is treating the audience as children who cannot understand the spoken word unless they also see it.

How should you use PowerPoint, if at all?

If some sort of a visual or mnemonic aid or leave-behind is expected, I suggest you skip PowerPoint entirely. Either before or after your presentation, give your audience a hard copy of your outline or key points and graphics.

If you decide to use PowerPoint—or simply can't resist the pressure—keep the number of slides and the amount of graphic ornamentation to a minimum.

You can use a short, bulleted outline to help your audience follow the main themes of your presentation. I suggest you put the entire outline on the screen, because the buildup of bullets can be distracting, as the audience waits to see what the next one will be.[3]

If some sort of pictorial or graphic representation of your words will help the audience understand what you're

3. I am indebted for this point to Elliot M. Perlman, MD (personal communication).

191

talking about (please, no pie charts that show 1/3 vs. 2/3), you can put that on the screen as well.

To avoid insulting or condescending to your audience, your PowerPoint must complement and supplement—never repeat—the words coming out of your mouth. It should never take the focus from you for more than a moment. Dare to be minimal.

49. Improving Your Delivery

Public speaking has an undeserved reputation as a source of anxiety. But there's really very little to worry about. If you've adequately prepared, if you fully understand your audience and have carefully crafted your message, you'll be fine. Preparation is the key. (On the other hand, if you're actually phobic about public speaking, you need more help than I can give you.)

There are countless instructional materials on the technique and practice of oral delivery. If you think you need improvement, you should seek professional help, either from an individual or a book, audio, or video.

How do you know if you need help? First, read the following tips on oral delivery.

Tips on Oral Delivery

These tips are the most relevant, in my experience.

Watch your posture. Check yourself in the mirror. Stand sideways and notice whether you hunch your back or stand with your head pitched in front of your shoulders. Too many people walk around with their head or shoulders thrust forward and are completely unaware that they're doing it.

Correct posture will make you seem taller and more persuasive and will allow you to breathe more freely. There are other health benefits as well.

When you speak, draw air from your abdomen. Almost no one does (except for professional speakers), but breathing from the diaphragm is a very simple technique that enables you to send much more air up through your vocal cords and greatly strengthen your voice and speaking endurance.

It's no harder to learn than walking and chewing gum at the same time. Just extend your abdomen as if you were demonstrating what a potbelly is ... and at the same time inhale through your nose. You'll feel the air flowing down into the lower lobes of your lungs. Now breathe continuously through your nose in this manner, inhaling by drawing air to your abdominal region and exhaling by flattening your stomach.

This breathing method will also relax you before speeches and ensure that your voice comes out strong, not thin and reedy. And it will enable you to project your voice to the back of the room the way actors do, without straining or shouting.

Since you're reading a book of perfect phrases, I assume that you'll be using a script or at least an outline into which the perfect phrases will be inserted. Ensure that your script or outline is printed out in the largest possible type that you can read comfortably.

I also assume you'll be using a lectern. Don't lean on it—or grasp it for dear life, as some speakers do. You can rest your hands lightly on the lectern (but don't twitch your hands or fingers in mini-gestures), or you can hold them at your sides, or you can gesture with one or both of them—whatever feels natural—or put one hand in your pocket (resist jingling your change or keys) and rest the other on the lectern, or hold a pen or a pointer, thus giving one hand something to do.

Do one or more of the above. Just avoid grasping, leaning, twitching, and jingling.

In general, keep your hands quiet: don't touch your face or tie knot, play with your glasses, or brush your hair back from your face. Such gestures convey nervousness. Your hands can reinforce what you're saying through gesture, but otherwise they should stay tastefully out of your speech.

Eye contact is important. Look directly at the audience or sweep your gaze across the audience. Occasionally look directly at one individual. Many speakers shy away from these kinds of eye contact, but in doing so they're giving up an effective means of connection. You can also look at a point directly beyond the last row of listeners, but don't do that for long stretches, much less the entire speech. You'll seem to be disengaged, and that's not good.

Practice your script or outline until you can deliver it conversationally. That means *acting out* the emotions in the script, which is why I'm constantly urging injecting the personal element—it gives you a chance to be a human being.

Your presentation style will be that of newscasters (with their excellent diction and subtle facial emotions) or of such limited-range actors as Kevin Costner and Keanu Reeves, who always play themselves, but with the appropriate emotions.

Turn up your intensity and your volume a little. Be your most persuasive self.

Another model: standup comics. Note the way they interact with audiences and hold their attention. Note especially the comic's skillful use of timing, pacing, and pauses.

Remember: energy. Never lapse into a singsong reading of your speech. Keep your delivery natural. Always act out your lines authentically. Make sure you bring to the task as much physical energy as is required. (If necessary, have a strong cup of coffee before you go up there.) Acting out with your face and eyes is especially important in video presentations, which typically focus on you from the shoulders up.

Don't drink too much alcohol or talk too much before

your speech. Have a glass of water inside the lectern. Make sure in advance that the microphone works. Provide an introduction of yourself if the introducer doesn't already have one.

Respect your listeners. Watch them for feedback. You can learn to distinguish inattention, forced attention, and real attention: note-taking and facial reactions to what you're saying are good signs; tapping PDAs and playing with coffee spoons are not. Never exceed your time limit. Make your listeners feel that their time was well spent.

That's about it. Next ....

Assess Yourself

Record your next speech on audio or video (preferably video):

Watch or listen to it critically, with the above advice in mind. If your self-analysis reveals that you're deficient in a particular area, you might want to work on the problem(s) yourself—or seek outside help.

About the Author

Alan Perlman received his bachelor's degree from Brown University and his master's and doctoral degrees from The University of Chicago. All three are in linguistics (the scientific study of language), with an emphasis on the history, grammar, sounds, meanings, and use of English. For 12 years, Alan taught linguistics and English composition at various colleges and universities, most recently at Wayne State University in Detroit. From 1981-2002 he was an executive speechwriter at Burroughs Corporation (now Unisys), General Motors, and Kraft Foods, where he developed speeches, articles, video scripts, and other high-level management communications. He is the author of numerous articles and four books on writing. Alan is currently a freelance writer, speech writer, and communications consultant. Visit his Web site at www.alanperlman.com.